Major Figures in the History of the OPW

Celebrating 175 years

Desmond McCabe

Published in 2006 by
Government Publications
The Office of Public Works
51 St Stephen's Green
Dublin 2

© The Office of Public Works 2006
ISBN 0-7557-7418-3

Text by Desmond McCabe (OPW History Project)
Edited by Elizabeth Mayes
Picture research by Elizabeth Mayes
Design and layout by Paul Martin Communications
Printed by Brunswick Press, Dublin (on 100%
recycled paper)

Commissioned by the OPW 175 Ideas Committee:
Angela Rolfe - Chair
Liam Basquille
Tom Bolger
Dermot Burke
George Moir
June Thompson

The text has been produced in co-operation with the OPW
History Project, with the kind assistance of Vincent
Campbell and Anne O'Shea.

**For their generous help with illustrations, special
thanks to:**
Donal O'Donovan; John J O'Sullivan; Tony Roche
(Dept. of Environment, Heritage and Local Government);
Denis McCarthy (Dublin Castle); Liam Furlong; Brendan
Rooney (National Gallery of Ireland); Valerie Ingram,
Nuala Canny and Conor Agnew (OPW Library); John
Callanan (Institution of Engineers of Ireland Library);
Anne Henderson and Simon Lincoln (Irish Architectural
Archive); Helen ní Cheallaigh (Clondalkin Public
Library); Joanna Finegan (National Library of Ireland);
and staff of the National Photographic Archive and the
UCD Delargy Centre for Irish Folklore.

Baile Átha Cliath
Arna fhoilsiú ag Oifig an tSoláthair
Le ceannach díreach ón
Oifig Dhíolta Foilseachán Rialtais, Teach Sun Alliance,
Scráid Theach Laighean, Baile Átha Cliath 2,
nó tríd an bpost ó
Foilseacháin Rialtais, An Rannóg Post-Tráchta, 51 Faiche
Stiabhna, Baile Átha Cliath 2,
(Teil: 01 - 6476834/35/36/37; Fax 01 - 6476843)

Dublin
Published by the Stationery Office
To be purchased directly from the
Government Publications Sale Office, Sun Alliance House,
Molesworth Street, Dublin 2,
or by mail order from
Government Publications, Postal Trade Section, 51 St.
Stephen's Green, Dublin 2,
(Tel: 01 - 6476834/35/36/37; Fax: 01 - 6476843)

Contents

Introduction

This year marks the 175th anniversary of the establishment of the Office of Public Works - (OPW). On October 15th 1831, the OPW came into being under a piece of legislation entitled "An Act for the Extension and Promotion of Public Works in Ireland".

In celebrating this 175th anniversary it is appropriate that we remember and acknowledge the people who have worked in the OPW in past times and pay tribute to them and to their accomplishments. This is the main reason behind the commissioning of this publication. By focusing on a number of major figures in the history of the OPW it provides an opportunity to present the great diversity and scale of works undertaken since its establishment.

The individuals selected represent different facets and eras of the OPW's work and by highlighting their contributions provides us with a condensed history of the Office. The other main criterion for selection was that those chosen were, as far as possible, different in background, personality and achievement. What we get are eight diverse figures, each with different skills, talents, interests and ambitions. What they share, however, is their great commitment to public service and a magnificent contribution to the development of our country.

John Fox Burgoyne

1782 - 1871

First Chairman of the Commissioners of Public Works in Ireland, 1831-45.
(Courtesy The Institution of Engineers of Ireland)

John Fox Burgoyne chaired the Office of the Commissioners of Public Works from its inception on 15th October 1831 until he resigned in June 1845. He was an immensely impressive figure. As military engineer he stood at the head of his profession and as civil administrator he displayed a rigorous grasp of organisational needs, together with a fine sense of empathy with his colleagues and a genuine and uplifting sense of mission in the public service. He was a man of action with an acute and practical intelligence. Somehow this was combined with a surprising and disarming want of aggression in the matter of self-advancement. If this was a weakness, it gave him a compensating insight into social psychology and values. He could be said to have got the Office of Public Works off to a very good start.

Son of a General, educated at Eton

Born in Soho, London, on 24th July 1782, he was the eldest of the four illegitimate children of Lt-General John Burgoyne (1723-92), a dashing, impetuous soldier, politician and light dramatist, and Susan Caulfield, a popular singer. His father had been excoriated in parliament for the collapse of a weakened British army under his command at Saratoga in October 1777, but later proved the integrity of his judgement.

When he died suddenly in 1792, Lt-General Burgoyne left an estate burdened with debt. One of his oldest friends, however, Edward Stanley, 12th Earl of Derby, took the children and their mother under his wing. He provided for Burgoyne's education at Eton and the Royal Military Academy at Woolwich (the prime training college for officers in the Royal Engineers). In the circumstances, Burgoyne was brought up as something of an outsider on the periphery of aristocratic circles: he was not obviously embittered by his situation and gained an unconventional vantage-point from which to look at class and society. He was gazetted second lieutenant in the Royal Engineers in 1798.

Military career abroad

During the Napoleonic Wars he served in Malta, including the siege of Valletta where he got his first promotion, in 1800; in Sicily; and in Egypt, where he was noticed by Sir John Moore for bravery and sound calculation at Alexandria and at the siege of Rosetta.

As commanding engineer attached to the 3rd or Light Division in the Peninsular War in Portugal in 1808, he took part in the ill-fated march into Spain. Buying time for the force in the retreat, John Fox Burgoyne expertly demolished several bridges. (Being so close to the detonations deafened him greatly for the next five years and indeed had lasting effect). He served later under General Arthur Wellesley (later the Duke of Wellington), who was appalled by his daring runs across the trenches in the siege of San Sebastian in 1813. It was said that 'Burgoyne was the wonder of us all; he seemed to bear a charmed life, for he was almost ever in the trenches, mines and lodgements'.

In December 1814, some months after the first abdication of Napoleon, Burgoyne accompanied the disastrous expedition to New Orleans, one of the last acts in the short Anglo-American war. To his chagrin, he missed the battle of Waterloo in July 1815.

1828: Engineer in Portsmouth

In 1821 he met and married Charlotte Rose (d.1870), daughter of Hugh Rose of Holme, Inverness, Scotland, and was made commanding engineer at Chatham. After further service in Portugal, in April 1828 he was appointed commanding engineer at Portsmouth where he made the acquaintance of Jacob Owen, later first Chief Architect of the OPW.

1831: Appointed first Chairman of the new Board of Public Works in Ireland

The new Board of Works (or the Office of Public Works) was established under legislation on 15th October 1831 in order to amalgamate the duties of the various bodies dealing from the late 18th century with aspects of state engineering, financial and architectural responsibilities. Provision was made for him to take the position of Chairman on secondment from the Royal Engineers: in fact he continued semi-automatically to climb the military ranks during the 1830s.

There is every indication that the opportunity was more than a random assignment and that he had been drawn towards such a role: he claimed in September 1831 to have 'often considered the anomaly which Ireland presents to the world - a fine country, possessed of many natural advantages…and yet eternally torn by faction…distress and turbulence'.

Though he was a fifty-year old be-medalled (and much wounded) veteran of the Napoleonic Wars, he was lucky to have been gifted with astonishing constitutional fitness and showed great suppleness and clarity of mind. It is obvious that he saw the position as a social responsibility rather than merely welcome bureaucratic employment. He refused to make idle assumptions about the country and visited Ireland in September 1831 to get a feel of conditions before he started work and as a precaution against his being 'warped by prejudice and party feeling'.

Burgoyne's impressions of Ireland

In a first encounter with Kingstown Harbour he was moved by the sight of ragged women grieving for the loss of husbands and brothers held under sentence of transportation in a convict ship. The 'open level' thoroughfares of Dublin and 'the grandeur of its public buildings' struck him forcibly by contrast with the frightening 'mass of beggars' in the city and the negligence of the better-off. His letters show that he was not at any point the prisoner of current clichés of interpretation. There were no undeserving poor, in his opinion. Wages were much lower than they should be in an expensive city like Dublin. If hucksters and shopkeepers cut corners selling poor commodities, it

seemed ultimately to arise from the ruthless advantage taken of the retail trade by the secure and propertied class. Burgoyne's sympathies were clearly with the 'shrewd, good-natured, inoffensive and industrious' poor and there was no trace of condescension or righteous indignation in his views.

After Dublin he journeyed to Limerick and, like most English and foreign travellers, he was staggered by the pauperised condition of the 'great mass of the population' in the countryside. In the usual way he stopped and interviewed farmers and labourers as to their means of livelihood. The 'fervent thanks' of destitute families for the gift of 'a miserable sixpence or shilling' Burgoyne found 'humiliating and heart-rending'. But, beyond any impressionistic sense of peasant degradation, he developed an understanding of the mechanisms of the landed estate and the local economy in rural Ireland. He diagnosed the causes of such distress and depression to be the inequities of the landlord-tenant relationship and the result of an enveloping 'system' (but one open to economic reason and political intervention) rather than wilful neglect or malice on the part of the landed gentry.

Prescription for economic recovery

His prescription for economic recovery was for public works properly managed under conditions of increased tenurial security and encouragement, better wages and lower rents. It was not simple-minded or orthodox and probably dismayed the bulk of politicians and landowners. Burgoyne started work by thinking out the realisable objectives of the new department. His ideas resembled a kind of Tory interventionism becoming increasingly old-fashioned as laissez-faire took hold of economics from the early 1800s.

Priorities of the new Board of Works

The Public Works Act passed in Westminster on 15th October 1831; he was formally appointed Chairman of the Board of Works with fellow-commissioners Brook Taylor

Kingstown (now Dun Laoghaire) Harbour. Interested in works involving explosives, Burgoyne improved the safety of the underwater works at the Harbour and at Dalkey quarry. (National Library of Ireland)

The Discovery of the Potato Blight in Ireland. McDonald's painting was done in 1847. Burgoyne chaired the Relief Commission for the distribution of aid at the peak of the Great Famine. (Courtesy UCD Delargy Centre for Irish Folklore)

Ottley and John Radcliff by the Lords of the Treasury on 1st November 1831 and called the first meeting of the Board for the following day. The Board met in the Merrion Street offices formerly occupied by the Directors General of Inland Navigation. One of its first priorities was to secure the transfer of documentation from the obsolete boards it was to replace and this was carried out satisfactorily over the winter. For most of the first year the Board met daily to further the transition and to set up loan and works procedures, while undertaking the regular business of maintenance and upkeep of the offices of state.

Having postponed consideration of numerous applications for works loans, the Board received Treasury approval in early December 1831 for their draft set of rules and regulations under which the loans were to be administered and had numbers printed for public use. In February 1832 Burgoyne convened surveying engineers in the early stages of the project that turned into the Shannon Commission. The key subordinate posts in the Board of Works were filled by the early summer of 1832. Among the early activities of the Board were tidying up the disarray in accounts due for relief roads undertaken by Alexander Nimmo in the west and coming to terms with the longstanding debts incurred by fishermen borrowing from the Fishery Board in the late 1820s (Burgoyne advised and got these debts cancelled). Burgoyne and the other commissioners were soon immersed in the distribution of public works loans.

Proposals for best use of loan fund

There is little doubt that he was a strong-minded chairman and felt no particular need to allow himself to be 'trained in' by his experienced colleagues. Burgoyne felt that the best use of the loan fund would be to 'make large advances for some descriptions of work' rather than dole out numerous small amounts for works of neutral or indifferent value. He argued that the loan fund should be increased and that the framework of the legislation of 1831 needed amendment. Knowing the critique developed by him in 1831, there was some irony and frustration in his comment in April 1835 that 'I am told by monied and mercantile men that the measure has been of great service'. In order of importance he placed loans for roads 'through uncultivated districts'; railways; 'leading lines of navigation like the Shannon'; harbours, canals and 'small fishery piers'; works 'not within the capability of private individuals' and for which 'the benefits would be so diffused over the whole body of the community, that the state alone would receive decided and immediate returns from them' (i.e. everyone would profit). Board of Works reports throughout the 1830s and early 1840s sound these topics strongly.

Safety in use of explosives

In 1835 Burgoyne became founder and first president for a decade of the Society of Civil Engineers of Ireland (which became the Institution of Civil Engineers of Ireland in 1844); it met for the first time at the offices of the Board of Works in the Custom House on 6th August that year. He frequently examined works going on in the Dublin area, particularly at Kingstown Harbour. It seems that he took special interest in works (roads and harbours often) where explosives were regularly handled. The safety record at Dalkey quarry and in the underwater works at Kingstown Harbour greatly improved during the 1830s on account of his re-evaluation of procedures being carried out in blasting. He was concerned to ascertain in great detail how to bring about the most effective and least dangerous detonations (on the intuitive supposition that the cleaner the explosion the more muted the noise) and expertly applied his military experience to the civil needs in public works.

1836: The new Railway Commission

By the mid-1830s the Viceregal government had become a little wary of his views: when the Railway Commission was set up in 1836 to advise on the development of Irish railways, moves were made to ensure that Burgoyne would not be made chairman and dominate the inquiry. But as the most active and knowledgeable of the Commissioners, Burgoyne largely drafted the report presented in 1838 and strongly influenced the finding of the Commission in favour of state control.

1845: Retires as Chairman of Board of Works

As Chairman of the Board of Works he expected a lot of his subordinates, for the greater good, but he was very much concerned with fairness of remuneration and 'esprit de corps'. His military maxims emphasised the overriding importance of 'system' having gone wrong whenever individual initiative and goodwill became paralysed. In spite of his military seniority no one could have less resembled the stock figure of the army 'blimp'.

He may have experienced some sense of defeat by the early 1840s as it became evident that there was going to be little alteration in the legal framework under which the loan fund was managed and that the sense of possibility in the air during the 1830s was being closed down. When in June 1845 he was offered the post of Inspector-General of Fortifications, he retired from the Chairmanship of the Board of Works and accepted it with little hesitation. In this capacity he assumed command of the Royal Engineers and sappers. Though he remained at the head of the Royal Engineers until retiring in 1868, he was extraordinarily active on commissions, inquiries and even, once more, in the field of war.

1847: The Relief Commission

Between February and September 1847 Burgoyne chaired the reorganised Relief Commission in charge of the distribution of food and the management of soup kitchens as the crisis of the Great Famine reached a peak. The success of his chairmanship was attributed to his 'intimate knowledge of Ireland and the confidence with which he is regarded in that country' together with his diplomacy and 'excellent judgement' in the management of frayed personalities prone to 'grumbling and declamation' in face of the back-breaking administrative work of keeping the Commission going, while under threat from critics in the Treasury, in Westminster and from internal squabbling. However, although Burgoyne timed his concluding report from the Relief Commission on 12th October 1847 (based on the collective governing fiction that the famine had ended) to coincide with an indignant private letter to The Times insisting that 'absolute famine still stares whole districts in the face', it remains puzzling that no other fiery outburst on his part against administrative complacency and parsimony is recorded. Such correspondence may be buried in unpublished state papers.

Engineering work 1848-68

Between 1848 and 1868 Burgoyne was occupied on inquiries into the new palace of Westminster, engineering flaws in the Caledonian canal, the proposed removal of the old Westminster bridge, the transatlantic packet stations commission, the commission on army promotion and on army inventions, metropolitan sewerage, the various great exhibitions of 1851, 1856 and 1862, postal developments, civil service rationalization and the coastal defence of Britain.

High command in Crimean War

During the Crimean war (1853-56) he ended up virtually second-in-command of the forces under Lord Raglan and in 1868 was made a Field-Marshal. He was made a baronet in 1856. As a man in his seventies he happily slept rough and rode without fatigue through the campaign. He retained his good health until the last year of his life.

Funeral panegyric

The panegyric at his funeral summed up his heroic and lovable character with more accuracy than is usual in these things: 'his kind and gentle manner…and his utter unselfishness, won the affection of all who became

The Dublin Crimean Banquet 22 October 1856. In the Custom House bonded warehouse (Stack A) 5,000 soldiers, seamen and guests celebrated the end of the war. (Illustrated London News, 8 November 1856. Courtesy National Library of Ireland)

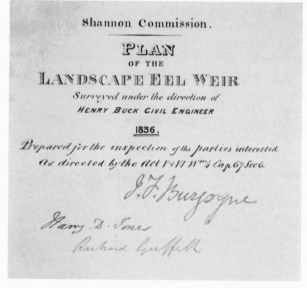

Signature of John Fox Burgoyne, 1836, on a plan of the landscape eel weir for the Shannon Commission.

associated with him. No one ever applied to him for assistance without receiving kind sympathy and as much aid as it was in his power to bestow. He was remarkable for his fondness for children and animals and an act of cruelty to one or the other was the only thing that could ruffle his temper…his modest and unassuming character was a drawback to his advancement…the Duke of Wellington understood him well when he said, "if Burgoyne only knew his own worth, there would be no one equal to him"…controversy or disputation were odious to him; even in pointing out to a man that he was wrong in argument, he did it so as not to lower him in his own estimation'.

Commemorated in London

The death of his only son, Hugh Talbot Burgoyne (1833-70, one of the first to be awarded a VC) on 7th September 1870 in naval trials in the Bay of Biscay shattered his morale and he died 'a complete wreck of his former self' on 7th October 1871. He is buried in the Tower of London and is commemorated in a statue raised at Waterloo Place, London.

John Burgoyne, *Ireland in 1831: Letters on the State of Ireland* (Dublin, 1831); Minutes of Board of Works, 1831-33 (OPW Library); Annual Reports of the Board of Works, 1832-1845; *First and Second Reports from the Select Committee Appointed to Inquire into the Amount of Advances made by the Commissioners of Public Works of Ireland with the Minutes of Evidence*, House of Commons, London, 1835 (379,573)XX; John Burgoyne, *Blasting and Quarrying* (Dublin, c.1839); George Wrottesley (ed.), *The Military Opinions of Sir John Fox Burgoyne* (3 vols., London, 1859); George Wrottesley, *The Life and Correspondence of Field-Marshal Sir John Fox Burgoyne* (2 vols, London, 1873); J.K.L., 'Hugh Talbot Burgoyne' in *National Dictionary of Biography* (London, c.1890); H.M.S., 'Sir John Fox Burgoyne' in *National Dictionary of Biography* (London, c.1890); John Berkery, John Fox Burgoyne, *Ireland's Own* (22 February 1991); Joseph Robins, *Custom House People* (Dublin, 1993); David Chandler, *Dictionary of the Napoleonic Wars* (Ware, 1999); Robin Haines, *Charles Trevelyan and the Great Irish Famine* (Dublin, 2004); John Sweetman, 'Sir John Fox Burgoyne' in *Oxford Dictionary of National Biography* (Oxford, 2004-06); Ann Martha Rowan, *Biographical Index of Irish Architects*, Irish Architectural Archive (1998-2006); Richard Hawkins, 'John Fox Burgoyne' in Royal Irish Academy's *Dictionary of Irish Biography* (Cambridge University Press, forthcoming).

Jacob Owen
1778 - 1870

First Chief Architect of the Office of Public Works 1832-56.
(Courtesy Irish Architectural Archive)

Jacob Owen was one of the dominant personalities of the Board of Works in its opening phase of development. He has perhaps been an underestimated figure in that the expression of a robust and controlling temperament in his conduct of the politics of office has distracted attention from the completion of much solid architectural work and the production of some subtle and interesting designs carried out in the 1830s and 1840s in public and private commissions.

Born and educated in Wales

Owen was born 28th July 1778 in Llanfihangel, in the mountains of north Montgomeryshire, mid-Wales (near Welshpool), son of Jacob Owen, civil engineer, and Margaret (Ellis) Owen. After secondary education boarding in Monmouth, he was taken pupil to the canal engineer William Underhill of the industrial 'Black Country' village of Tipton, Staffordshire. It is likely he put in five years apprenticeship to Underhill and got a broad and thorough experience in the manner of the time, after which (perhaps around 1798, when he married Mary Underhill, his master's daughter) he moved to London where it is conjectured that he was employed by Thomas Bush, surveyor.

1805: Engineer in Portsmouth

Bush may have used contacts in the Board of Ordnance to help Owen secure a civilian post on the staff of the Royal Engineers at Portsmouth in July 1805. He and his wife would have already been well into the creation of a household that was eventually to comprise 17 children: it is not surprising that much of his energies went into providing for such a large brood. He was promoted permanent clerk of works in 1806. Virtually his entire career in the Royal Engineers was passed at Portsmouth where he probably assisted in the defensive fortification of the south coast of England during the Napoleonic wars and designed offices and warehouses in the naval dockyards. Though only some of his later English commissions are

known for sure, it is certain that Owen cultivated a private business in Portsmouth in addition to his public office from 1805-06 (this was by no means unusual).

The public office was itself something of a collaboration between Owen and his brother John (d.1867). In his latter years at Portsmouth Owen specialised (with his son Trevor Ellis Owen, 1804-62) in the design of churches and schools. In 1827 he took over the handling of a church at Bembridge, Sussex, relinquished by the celebrated John Nash, which had unfortunately to be demolished in 1845, following irreparable structural failure.

Friendship with Burgoyne

Between 1828 and 1831 Owen forged a warm relationship with John Fox Burgoyne, recently appointed Colonel commanding the Royal Engineers at Portsmouth. Whatever Owen's reputation in the Board of Works in the latter years of his tenure, the fact that he had the wholehearted confidence of such a capable and sterling character as Burgoyne suggests a core of integrity and virtue. In 1831, Burgoyne had been appointed Chairman of the newly established Board of Public Works in Ireland, and between October that year and the summer of 1832 he and his fellow Commissioners were engaged in setting up procedures of office and in rounds of appointment to the initially small permanent staff.

1832: Appointed Chief Architect in new Board of Works

Though William Murray, formerly assistant architect to Francis Johnston (d.1830) in the old Board of Works (and some ten years junior to Owen), supposed that the new post of Chief Architect was his for the taking, he reckoned without the strenuous exertions of Burgoyne on behalf of his former associate. The new Board swept aside Murray's pretensions to office in April 1832 in correspondence with the Viceregency. On 9th May 1832 Owen was formally recommended to a post uniting 'the two situations of engineer and architect' on the strength of

The Coach House at Dublin Castle, designed by Jacob Owen, 1833-34, the 'charming Gothic crenellations harmonising with Francis Johnston's 1816 Chapel Royal'.

The Dublin Metropolitan Police Barrack, Dublin Castle, designed by Jacob Owen in 1838. (Drawing by Pat Liddy, reproduced by courtesy of the artist).

Burgoyne's knowledge of his 'abilities and integrity' and seemingly reinforced by the goodwill of the Lord Lieutenant, the Marquis of Anglesey, and Sir William Gosset, Under-Secretary 'who were both well acquainted with him previously'. This was an unbeatable combination and indeed Burgoyne never wavered in his support, asserting roundly in April 1835 that Owen was 'the most able man for the situation I ever knew in my life'.

Owen's extensive duties 1832-46

Receiving a salary of £800 per annum for his public duties, for the first fourteen years of his term in office (that is until August 1846) Owen also ensured that he was 'avowedly permitted to accept private engagements'. The arrangement ceased as the Board buckled under the strain of Famine Relief. During the 1830s his duties were summed up as 'the whole of the engineer's and architect's business in Dublin, a general but less direct superintendence of various works in the country and answering references and consultations on other points of sufficient importance'. This embraced a monitoring and advisory role in the case of the many projects funded largely by the Board of Works, some of it desk-bound but much requiring visits around the country.

Owen's highly competent protégés

He had no official aid in his professional capacity but, according to the contemporary pattern of apprenticeship training, had a number of students in the office of the Board answerable directly to him. These included Charles Lanyon (1813-89) who probably came over with him from Portsmouth, and who later became his son-in-law; Thomas Turner, son of Richard Turner, the Dublin ironmaster; Richard Williamson, and several of his own sons. His habit was to see to it that these pupils later obtained the pick of whatever professional patronage was going in return for their loyalty. Though this was widely resented, there is no doubt that it was the way of the world at the time and that his protégés were invariably highly competent: his critics would have done much the same in his position. There was no hint of financial corruption in the administration of the architectural department of the Board of Works between 1831 and 1856.

His own work for the Board was understated on the whole but consistently well-formed, from the evidence extant. Early on he made some alterations to plans in the works ongoing at the Carlow courthouse and at a bridge over the River Lagan near Belfast: it is likely that he had some input into many of these publicly-financed (by loan or grant or both together) works.

Dublin Castle improvements 1833-49

The stables and coach-house at Dublin Castle were designed in a charming Gothic crenellation in 1833-34 in order to harmonise with the architecture of the Royal Chapel (Francis Johnston, 1816). The Dublin Metropolitan Police Barrack (of 1838) in the Castle was styled to conform to Thomas Eyre's mid-18th century house. A cavalry guard-house and riding-school were erected according to Owen's designs at Dublin Castle in 1837. His carriage-office of 1838 in Dublin Castle manifested Owen's instinctive leaning to neo-Classical simplicity.

Additions to Phoenix Park and Viceregal Lodge

Owen made additions to the Chief Secretary's office in 1840-41. Between 1838 and 1849 Owen was required at various times to remodel the State Apartments. The so-called 'battle-axe staircase' was renewed with the fine ornamental ironwork of Richard Turner (a favourite contractor of Owen's at many venues). In a piece of engineering that was of sufficient economy and grace to warrant special discussion at the Institution of Civil Engineers of Ireland, Owen in 1849 raised the roof of the Presence Chamber, to improve ventilation in the room and to heighten its 'architectural character', by hoisting the roof framework (stripped of mouldering slates) as one unit

The Viceregal Lodge (1831) now Aras an Uachtarain. Jacob Owen designed extensions to the Viceregal Lodge for visits from Queen Victoria in 1843 and 1849. (Engraved from a drawing by George Petrie RHA, National Library of Ireland)

The 'Battle-Axe Staircase' in the State Apartments, Dublin Castle, designed by Jacob Owen c. 1840s, with ironwork by Richard Turner.

on a set of well-balanced screw-jacks, rather than undertake the tedious job of 'taking asunder and refixing all the timbers'.

Owen played a significant executant role in landscaping the Phoenix Park according to the grand designs of Decimus Burton in the 1830s and the 1840s. One deer-keeper's lodge, a cottage orné, has been attributed to him. He made very significant additions to the Viceregal Lodge, erecting coachhouses in 1842, enlarging and reshaping the rooms of the east wing in several steps between 1843 and 1849 in time for the visit of Queen Victoria. A triple-arched entrance gate and a ballroom were among his contributions to the Chief Secretary's Lodge in 1845. Between 1840 and 1843 Owen, with the Carolin brothers (with whom he had close ties), designed and built the plain but well-balanced Police Depot at the north-eastern edge of the Phoenix Park. All the signs are that his preferences were for a simple and undemonstrative Greek Revival architecture: this may indicate that his imaginative reach was not of the highest order but that he designed very well within such limitations. (His coat of arms displayed an Ionic order).

Work on the Four Courts, prisons and asylums

At the Four Courts in the mid-1830s and in the early 1840s Owen carried to conclusion a dignified plan for Benchers' and Solicitors' rooms and a coffee room (in accordance with the temperance crusade), a bankruptcy court and a new block containing Rolls Court, Admiralty Court, Nisi Prius Court and a galleried Law Library. Owen oversaw the construction of major new prisons and penitentiaries in Dublin and Belfast (Mountjoy in 1847-50). He also performed an important monitoring role in the erection of the seven district asylums built in Ireland during the 1840s - Killarney, Cork, Carlow, Ballinasloe, Sligo, Mullingar and Omagh.

He earned by 'working at all hours early & late with a good will' the steadfast regard of the Board of Commissioners before and after the departure of Burgoyne

At the Four Courts in Dublin in the 1830s and 1840s Owen carried out substantial 'dignified' developments. (Drawing by Fergus Ryan. Original in Irish Architectural Archive)

in 1845. There is no reason to doubt the verdict of his contemporaries as to his 'unbending honesty of character'.

The Queen's Colleges

Owen was charged with the supervision of the Queen's Colleges at Belfast, Galway and Cork and with the management of extensions to Maynooth College. He kept to himself the design and construction of the criminal lunatic asylum at Dundrum, County Dublin (1847-50). It is perhaps not unexpected that such ubiquity upset some of his competitors: in June 1838 there were scurrilous allegations that Owen and the Carolins, as Tories and Orangemen of long standing, defrauded the public by skimping in the construction of the Solicitors' Building at the Four Courts. But Owen scotched the accusations without difficulty and indeed, there is no reason to think that he was ever deeply moved by party politics.

Though he may have annoyed some of his fellows by his conduct and by his vocational success, it is equally true to say that he could, if he needed to, get on with almost everyone. In the later 1830s and in the 1840s he happily served on committee with his old rival, William Murray. He was more than a blindly self-interested nepotist (though he was certainly that in part) and was concerned that his sons and protégés establish wide and profitable professional connections.

Active in IAI and ICEI

He was circumstantially involved in the creation of the Irish Architectural Institute in 1839. Joining as soon as it came into being, he acted as vice-president from 1849 to 1866. He was perhaps more active at council level in the Institution of Civil Engineers of Ireland, serving on the council in 1845, 1847-50, 1852-54, and in 1857 and as vice-president in 1842-44, 1846, 1859 and 1861. Though he had clearly been guilty of favouritism in the examinations for County Surveyor for which the Board of Works had responsibility between 1834 and 1858, he escaped censure in a Treasury inquiry carried out in May 1856, just after he retired.

Succeeded by his son

His last act of nepotism, however, occurred as he had approached retirement that year: he could have called a halt to his employment in 1855 but he was reluctant to go until a re-grading of posts within the architectural department in 1856 enabled his son, James Higgins Owen (1824-91) to progress into his father's seat in office. (It was 1914 before the hold of the extended family on the Board of Works was finally extinguished).

Vigorous retirement 1856-70

Owen remained energetic and busy in retirement, finding 'the day is not long enough for what I find necessary to do, now that I am supposed to do nothing'. His vigour was undiminished for some time. In the 1860s he co-founded the Irish Civil Service Building Society (with his son, J.H. Owen) and continued a financial interest in the building speculations of T.E. Owen in Southsea, settling in 1867 for a short while, with his second wife, in the seaside resort. He must have retired again to the neighbourhood of his old in-laws in Staffordshire shortly afterwards, dying at Great Bridge, Tipton on 29th October 1870 and was transported to Dublin to be buried with his first wife in Mount Jerome. (His second wife died in April 1870). He was nothing if not a family man, leaving an estate worth some £20,000 for the provision of his heirs and dependants. From the point of view of the Board of Works, the commissions of state had been in good hands during his reign as principal architect.

Jacob Owen, 'An account of the mode adopted for raising the roof of the Presence Chamber, Dublin Castle', *The Transactions of the Institution of Civil Engineers of Ireland*, vol III, 1839, pp.32-34; 'Obituary', *Irish Builder*, 12th December 1870; Frederick O'Dwyer, 'The architecture of the Board of Public Works, 1831-1923', in John Regan & Ciaran O'Connor, *Public Works; the Architecture of the Office of Public Works, 1831-1987* (Dublin, 1987), pp.10-32; Joseph Robins, *Custom House People* (Dublin, 1993); Frederick O'Dwyer, 'Building empires: architecture, politics and the Board of Works, 1760-1860', *Irish Architectural and Decorative Studies*, vol.5, 2002, pp.108-175; Christine Casey, *Dublin: the city within the Grand and Royal Canals and the Circular Road with the Phoenix Park* (New Haven and London, 2005); Ann Martha Rowan, *Biographical index of Irish architects*, Irish Architectural Archive (1998-2006).

William Thomas Mulvany

1806 - 1885

Engineer in the Office of Public Works 1834-54.
(Courtesy J J O'Sullivan and Bildarchiv der Stadt Herne)

Mulvany was an extremely able and vigorous engineer who looked outside the narrow limits of his professional responsibilities towards the development of a comprehensive understanding of how technology and efficient enterprise might transform social conditions. During his career in the Board of Works (1834-54) he conceived of an ambitious project dramatically to increase Irish soil fertility by undertaking a systematic drainage of the country's rivers and streams: nothing like it had previously been tried in Europe. One of his misfortunes was that this had to be attempted in collaboration with a landowning class jealously resentful of real or imagined state infringement upon its property rights even during the tragedy of the Great Famine: a committee of the House of Lords brought Mulvany down in the end. Migrating to Düsseldorf in 1854, he proved his visionary brilliance and underlined the loss suffered through his departure, by Ireland and the Board of Works, by the leading role he took in the transformation of the Ruhr valley, within twenty years, from thinly-exploited scrub and forest to the industrial core of the new German state under Bismarck. A protégé and admirer of John Fox Burgoyne, he had also briefly been a pupil of the great Francis Johnston (1761-1830) and so formed a link in the 1830s and 1840s between the old Board of Works and the new.

Son of a gifted artistic family

He was born on 11th March 1806 in Sandymount, Dublin, eldest of seven children (five boys and two girls) of Thomas James Mulvany (1779-1845) and Mary (Field) Mulvany (d.1865 in Düsseldorf). His father, who was one of the principal inspirations in his life and career, somehow kept a bohemian household going by makeshift tutorial work and by getting odd commissions as painter and draughtsman. He was one of the founding members of the Royal Hibernian Academy (RHA) in 1823 and became its Keeper in 1841. Though most of his gifted family attained greater worldly and perhaps professional success than their father, none had his bravura or conversational magnificence.

All of the sons seem to have developed aspects of their father's talent. George Francis Mulvany (1809-69) followed in his steps as painter and member of the RHA, and became the first Director of the National Gallery of Ireland, which opened in 1864. John Skipton Mulvany (1813-70) turned out a very fine architect. Richard John became a publisher. The youngest child, Thomas John Mulvany (1821-95), came into the profession of engineering under the guidance of his oldest brother, joining the Board of Works in 1847 and moving to Germany in 1855.

Education and apprenticeship

Mulvany got to grips with draughtsmanship at home with his father and was educated at Dr Wall's school in Hume Street between c.1816 and 1822. He entered the school of medicine in Trinity College Dublin in June 1823 but had to abandon his studies after a few months when there was a setback to the family finances. It is likely that through his father's contacts he got work or experience in the office of Francis Johnston during the construction of the Abbey Street premises of the Royal Hibernian Academy in 1824-25. Afterwards he was accepted as pupil in the office of John Semple (d.1881), church architect. In late November 1826 he applied for a job as civilian draughtsman on the Ordnance Survey, getting one or two months work map-making around Coleraine before he was enabled to move to a slightly better paid position on the newly-augmented Boundary Survey under Richard Griffith.

Works on the Boundary Survey

It is clear that Mulvany now aimed, by December 1826, at a career in engineering and had begun seriously 'studying his profession' on his own account. The Boundary Survey entailed fixing townland, parish and baronial boundaries as a basis for the work of the Ordnance Survey. It suited Mulvany to stay in this post

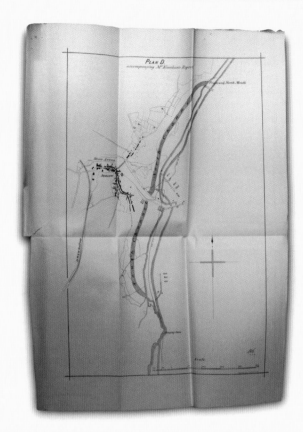

The rivers Shannon and Erne with the link planned by Mulvany in mid 19th century. Now the Shannon-Erne Waterway.

until the early 1830s when he seems to have picked up small jobs as an assistant in 'some engineering works in the west of Ireland'.

In Limerick, first engineering work

The first Shannon Navigation Act was passed in September 1835, authorising the Shannon Commission to appoint staff and plan for works to improve the river's navigation and drainage. Late in 1834, Mulvany was taken on as assistant engineer under Henry Buck, to deal under supervision with the Shannon estuary and the old Limerick Navigation. It is probably no coincidence that he also married in 1835, Alicia Winslow (1797-1886) of Clogher, County Tyrone, daughter of a small Catholic landowner. The couple settled in Limerick City, as Mulvany began his first major engineering job, work which was to establish him as an authority on arterial drainage.

Expert on Shannon Drainage 1830s

Burgoyne later recalled of Mulvany that 'he showed himself so able and many of his reports were so very good, he was so extremely zealous and so active' (having a particular aptitude for the key problem of drainage) that he came to the attention of the Commission and was promoted to the charge of the Upper Shannon survey in 1837. Apart from surveying the flood-plain of the Shannon, a lot of the immediate work involved gathering local knowledge of the flood-history of the river: Burgoyne later used a number of Mulvany's reports in the College of Royal Engineering at Woolwich 'as matters for instruction'.

Canals, bridges, quays and piers

The navigation works were finally given legislative sanction in August 1839 and Mulvany was shortly after appointed district engineer for the Lower Shannon. In the fashion of the time, he took on his youngest brother and his nephew as assistants and pupils.

Mulvany initiated the statutory process under which mills, fisheries and lands were valued and owners compensated for disturbance. He also designed a linking route by waterway from the Shannon to the Ulster Canal, via Belturbet in the Erne basin: the Ballinamore and Ballyconnell canal was later executed by his brother. Contractors were secured on the basis of finalised designs for works such as Ballylongford quay, Foynes harbour, Clarecastle quay, Kilrush pier, Athlunkard weir, a weir at Arthur's Ferry, excavations at O'Brien's Bridge, Killaloe Weir and the remodelling of Killaloe Bridge. With the exception of a wooden bridge at Plassey and the removal of a gravel shoal at Killaloe in the summer of 1841, little of this had even been commenced before Mulvany departed the Commission in late 1842.

1842: Drainage and Fisheries Acts

The shortcomings of the More O'Ferrall Act (1831) had become evident in the course of the work of the Shannon Commission and it appears that the improved Drainage Act of October 1842 was drafted early that year by the Treasury 'in concert with Sir John Burgoyne and Mr Mulvany'. The Act came into operation simultaneously with the Fisheries Act of 6 Vict c.106 which refashioned the archaic Irish fisheries legislation and placed the Board of Works in superintendence of river and sea stocks.

The issues of drainage and inland fisheries were tied together during the Shannon works and it seemed natural to make Mulvany 'principal agent' in both departments, being 'a man of great energy and considerable talent' and 'thorough knowledge of the details of both'. From October 1842 he acted as one of two inspectors of fisheries (the other being the redoubtable James Redmond Barry) on a salary of £200 per annum. This occupied a great deal of time in terms of general administration, the arbitration of disputes and the elucidation of public attitudes and habitual modes of river and sea fishing.

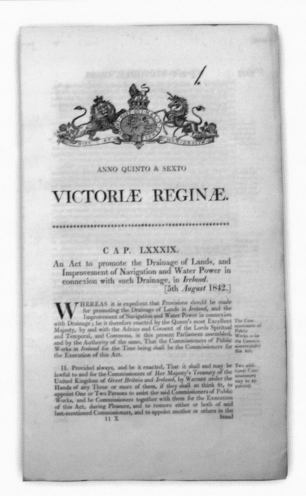

The Drainage Act of 1842. Mulvany's 'brainchild', advocated extensive arterial drainage works, not 'piecemeal reclamation of bogs'.

1846: Assistant Commissioner

In May 1844 Mulvany and Barry engaged in a massive public inquiry into game fishing seasons and the use and abuse of 'engines of capture' on Irish rivers. In May 1846 Mulvany was recommended on account of his record of 'zeal and activity' to be raised to Commissioner of Irish Fisheries, and accordingly, to junior or assistant Commissioner of the Board of Works (& Fisheries): the latter promotion was ratified by Treasury order in August 1846. During the Famine the enlarged department made a special effort, in a kind of public-private partnership, to get fish-curing depots going on the west coast of Ireland.

Though there were intractable problems in the management of Irish fisheries, Mulvany was never so hard-pressed as he was in the Department of Drainage. There, he was largely on his own. The Act of 1842 more than anything was his brainchild, reflecting the notion that the piecemeal reclamation of bogs was ineffectual in its contribution to Irish agriculture and best superseded by extensive and thoroughly planned works of arterial drainage.

Drainage schemes and property rights

The 1842 Act treaded very gingerly on matters of property rights. It was presented entirely as 'enabling in its principle, founded on the voluntary initiation of the parties interested' and in which the expertise of the 'Board of Public Works and its staff' was shared in the execution of large-scale works. There remained a nagging contradiction between voluntary choice and the need both for heroic country-wide planning in the extent and timing of works and the management of local opinion. The idea in 1842 was that interested landowners would co-operate in the Board's decision-making and contribute financially towards works on a particular river, to be carried out with consent of a two-thirds majority. In practice, however, between 1842 and 1845 landowners proved cautious and unforthcoming. Drainage works were undertaken in only six districts.

1845: Onset of Famine

With the onset of famine and severe distress in the autumn of 1845, the Tory government cast about for appropriate measures of relief. Mulvany argued in November that year that drainage schemes funded by the Treasury were 'peculiarly fitted to meet such an emergency as that anticipated, diffusing employment of a simple class'. And there is little doubt that the bulk of landowners welcomed drainage as a 'reproductive' rather than a 'useless' work: 'it was their money that was being expended and they preferred to have it laid out in improving their properties'.

Difficulties of drainage relief works

Under Treasury notice, Board surveys of important rivers were urgently commenced in late December 1845. The administrative process was streamlined, on Mulvany's advice, to enable the Board of Works to expedite the schemes in some 115 districts around the country. As it had been found relatively easy to obtain 50% landed approval of district schemes, the threshold for consent was reduced to half the relevant landownership. Initially the clamour for schemes was intense. Between 1845 and 1852 land belonging to over 3000 landowners was improved at a cost of almost £2m, nearly all of which came in the form of Treasury loans. Considerable numbers were given crucial relief work between 1847 and 1849. Mulvany and his battalion of subordinate engineers braved immense difficulties, in the midst of dire crisis, in the co-ordination and planning of hydraulic works unprecedented in their scale and complexity.

The schemes were dogged, however, by the repeated failure of Treasury loans to come on stream in time for necessarily seasonal works to proceed. And, more fundamentally, it was unjust and profoundly unreasonable to expect drainage works operating as means of relief in a time of starvation to be brought, during the crisis itself, to a fully functional state.

Landowners campaign to censure Mulvany

Many of the schemes worked well against all the odds. But others were not finished by 1850 and an angry rump of landowners, marshalled by William Parsons (1800-67), third earl of Rosse, campaigned specifically for the censure of Mulvany, as the architect of the drainage schemes, and for the abolition of Treasury charges on their lands. The nub of their case was the injustice perceived to have been done to Irish landowners by the modifications to the process of consent carried out in the Act of 1846.

Charles Trevelyan and C.H. Wood of the Treasury at first joined forces against Mulvany, fearing blame might be attached to their administration of drainage loans (they later took his side). As early as April 1850 Trevelyan probed (unsuccessfully) to see if allegations of corruption might be laid against Mulvany. Though there was no question of setting up a Commons inquiry, by April-May 1852 Rosse had roused the House of Lords and many Irish localities to some fury. One of Mulvany's district engineers warned him that most of the grand jury in King's County 'were totally unreserved in their remarks. What surprised me most was the feeling against yourself. To you…is attributed the alleged twisting and turning of the Acts'.

House of Lords Inquiry

A Lords Committee of Inquiry was established in early June 1852 summoning Mulvany to account for the alleged mismanagement of the Irish drainage. Though he defended himself stoutly with a detailed and analytical presentation of the evidence, the Lords Committee, in a confused and heavy-handed report that refused, among other things, to take account of the claims for relief pressing upon the works during the period from 1846 to 1850, chose to pin most of the blame for the heavy cost of works upon the Board of Works in the person of Mulvany. There was no punishment attached to the unjust sentence but the solemn roar of a Lords Committee still carried weight in Victorian society and Mulvany was made to feel the social disgrace.

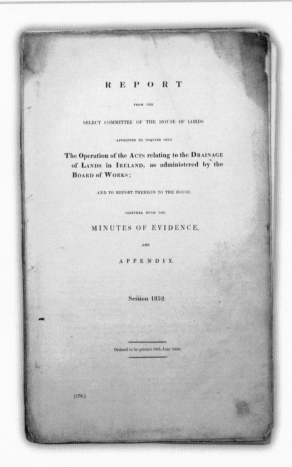

The Report from the House of Lords in 1852 which led to Mulvany's censure as architect of the drainage schemes and retirement on pension from the OPW in 1854.

The coalmines of Mulvany's company were the most advanced in Germany. The Erin mine, near Düsseldorf, closed in 1983 and is preserved as a memorial. (Courtesy J J O'Sullivan)

Mulvany introduced the Irish steeplechase to Germany and laid out a 3-mile course at his house in Castrop. (Courtesy J J O'Sullivan)

1854: Retirement

The Board of Works was morally weakened at a period of drastic retrenchment by the Treasury. And, not least, the land charges were quietly reduced. Mulvany was assigned two or three years in which to bring various outstanding works of drainage to completion (and his salary was raised!). But, though it is not clear that he was under pressure to resign, his health had suffered greatly during and after the Famine works. He took advantage of the terms of a recent Superannuation Act to retire in early 1854 on pension from the Board of Works.

'Astonishing reversal of ill-fortune' in Germany

The epilogue to his Board career, however, proved an astonishing reversal of ill-fortune. Moving to London he recuperated after a regimen of outdoor exercise and became interested, through friendship with an Irish-Belgian entrepreneur, in the prospect of coal-mining in the Ruhr valley, then something of a wilderness. Mobilising investment from Quaker contacts in Ireland and educating himself in the latest mining technology being employed in the deep pits of Durham and Northumberland, Mulvany hired English coal-mining experts, supervised the purchase of a promising claim at Gelsenkirchen near Dortmund and registered a company in Germany with his group of investors (holding a one-eighth share of the capital).

Successful mining in Ruhr Valley

Though the company was one of many staking claims in a newly-deregulated area of the (then) Prussian state, under the leadership of Mulvany, the 'Hibernia' mine (opened 17th March 1855) and its sister-mine, the 'Shamrock', proved vastly more efficient and successful than most. Within a couple of years these mines were recognised as among the most advanced in Germany and the techniques imported from England were being widely imitated. Mulvany presided over a business-federation (the Bergverein) which advised government agencies on the distribution of an emerging rail, road and canal network in the Ruhr and beyond, with the objective of creating an integrated industrial region, resembling the English midlands but this time consciously planned.

1885: Dies in Germany 'loaded with honours'

Having mastered spoken and written German, Mulvany produced, between 1860 and 1884, some 27 major studies of the evolving needs of the region. Incidentally, belying the apparent earnestness of his personality, he also introduced the Irish steeplechase to Germany, when he designed a course on the grounds of his estate at Castrop outside Düsseldorf in the early 1870s. Loaded with honours in Germany, he died on 30th October 1885 in his daughter's home in Düsseldorf. The Irish Times obituary that week made it 'a suggestive commentary on our system that long experience and abilities of a high order, which should have been devoted to the amelioration of this country and the development of its resources, were more highly prized and rewarded in a foreign land'.

Report from the Select Committee of the House of Lords appointed to inquire into the Operation of the Acts relating to the Drainage of Land in Ireland as administered by the Board of Works, House of Commons 1852-53 (10) xxvi; L.C., 'Thomas James Mulvany' in *Dictionary of National Biography* (London 1890-98); W.O. Henderson, 'W.T. Mulvany: an Irish pioneer in the Ruhr' in *Britain and Industrial Europe* (London, 1954); J. O'Loan, 'William Thomas Mulvany', *Administration*, viii (1960), 315-32; A.R.G. Griffiths, *The Irish Board of Works*, 1831-78 (1987); Joseph Robins, *Custom House People* (Dublin, 1993); James Dooge, 'Hibernia in Ruhrgebeit: William Thomas Mulvany and the Industrialisation of the Ruhr', *History Ireland*,vol. v, no.3 (Autumn 1997), 31-35; Olaf Schmidt-Rutsch, 'William Thomas Mulvany: ein irischer pragmatiker und visionär im Ruhrgebeit, 1806-1885' (PhD thesis, Ruhr-Universität Bochum, 2001); John J. O'Sullivan, *Breaking Ground: the story of William Thomas Mulvany* (Cork, 2003).

Robert Manning

1816 - 1897

Chief Engineer at the Board of Works 1874-91.
(Courtesy The Institution of Engineers of Ireland)

One of the advantages to being an engineer in the 19th century was that sweeping technological change and dramatic endeavours in the area of public works meant that new and uncharted fields of expertise opened up all the time. The early Victorian engineer, who had generally mastered his subject in the manner of an apprentice thrown into the practical difficulties of the discipline, had often to develop bold new solutions to problems as they arose. Robert Manning was one of the few who proved able to follow up workable successes on site with innovative mathematical analysis. His so-called 'monomial formula', published in 1889, satisfactorily summed up, in terms that have survived for over a century, a founding mathematical expression for determining the mean velocity of channel flow. This was a theoretical achievement of very great significance.

Born in British occupied France 1816

Robert Manning was born in Avincourt, Normandy on 22nd October 1816, the third son of William Manning (d.1826) of Knocknamohill, County Wicklow and Ruth Stephens (1792-1854), of Dromina, near Passage East, County Waterford. As adjutant in the 40th regiment of foot, his father was garrisoned in France during the British post-war occupation of 1814-18. It is not clear where the family lived between 1818 and his father's early death in November 1826 (he had languished since taking part in the battle of Waterloo), but it is likely that they settled, after military disbandment, on half-pay or pension in Wicklow.

Early life on Waterford Estate

After his father's death, the family lived in the maternal home on an estate (c.1000 acres) at Springhill, County Waterford. Manning grew up warmly attached to his uncle and picked up the rudiments of estate management, being the elements of surveying, draughtsmanship and book-keeping (and perhaps the basics of reclamation and field drainage), from Mr Muckleary, the farm steward. Getting to grips with the

mechanism of the Ballycanvan tidal corn-mill on the estate made a valuable preliminary to dealing with the many (and tricky) river mills he encountered on the drainage schemes of the 1840s and 1850s. Also, talking in the 1880s about problems of silting in Waterford harbour, he pointed out that he had been familiar with the currents and ways of the channel since boyhood.

Though it is evident from his first published work in the early 1850s that Manning must have gained a thorough grounding in applied mathematics and modern languages in school in Waterford and Kilkenny in the 1820s and 1830s, he did not proceed to Trinity College. As third in line potentially to the family estate (his uncle died childless in 1856), his future in small landownership looked tenuous. His mother's family, though on the very fringe of county society, had some useful connections but Manning made little headway in 1843-44, groping towards a career in law or as an officer in the police constabulary. His papers show that he was entirely at a loose end in late 1845 as famine loomed.

1846: Drainage engineer in Louth

At this juncture he was rescued when in January 1846 the prominent engineer, Samuel Usher Roberts, from Waterford City, secured him a temporary clerical post on the expanding drainage relief schemes under the Board of Works. It seems that he served creditably on the Glyde River works in County Louth for a couple of months before he was formally inducted on to the Drainage staff. Henry Paine, Board secretary, ratified his appointment unusually as 'accountant' and draughtsman, 'at the rate of two guineas per week' (c.£109 p.a.) on 27th April 1846. The brief included taking 'charge of the district engineer's office', minding site stores and 'such other duties as the engineer shall require'.

1848: Promoted to District Engineer

In the mounting disorder of famine works, Roberts (who must have known Manning) threw his clerk into the

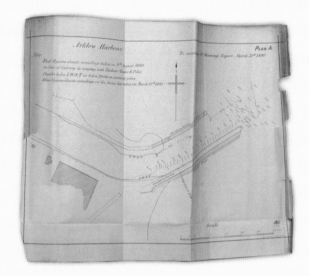

Arklow Harbour works. Manning constructed some one hundred piers and harbours. The excellence of his work on Arklow Harbour was highlighted.

management of sections of drainage, for which he must have been immediately capable, so that, by 1st October 1846, Manning had the confidence of his superior as an assistant engineer. It is curious how such a distinguished career owed its development to circumstantial accident.

In January 1847 the Board of Works formally promoted Manning to assistant engineer under Roberts on a range of drainage districts mostly in the counties of Meath and Louth, raising his wages to three guineas for a six-day week (c.£164 p.a.). As 'a good practical surveyor', the assistant engineer was expected to 'lay out the works on the ground strictly according' to plans furnished from the office of the District Engineer. In practice, overwhelmed by work, Roberts no doubt allowed Manning a good deal of practical leeway on site. This is suggested by the fact that in January 1848, when Roberts was transferred to County Galway and the management of the districts of Corrib and Turloughmore, Manning was appointed District Engineer on the Ardee and Glyde works (and five other lesser districts) in his place at a salary of £300 per annum.

Self-education in hydrology

This gave Manning the wherewithal to marry Susanne Gibson (1818-94) of Baggot St, Dublin in March 1848: the couple rented Annagassan Lodge, on the Glyde, Co. Louth while Manning was engaged full-time on the drainage works, and produced four girls and four boys between 1849 and 1864. In spite of the arduous pressures of the works (and children), Manning rapidly educated himself to a high theoretical level in hydrology, devouring as a 'beginner', the *Traité d'Hydraulique* published in 1840 by M d'Aubisson de Voisons, the then authority on the subject. As a newcomer he must surely have excelled in his early mathematical studies to have been able to rise to such a challenge.

He was guided by Robert Mallet whom he would have known from the Institution of Civil Engineers of Ireland to which Manning had been elected associate member in 1848. As District Engineer he no longer had Roberts to lean on while figuring out the convolutions of estuary and flood behaviour. The preservation of working water-powered mills on rivers undergoing drainage treatment was one of the recurrent difficulties he faced. Due to the unpredictability of the weather and for reasons of bureaucracy, Manning had also to be prepared to halt and pick up operations irregularly without losing forward momentum in the works.

Difficulties of Glyde river scheme

The Glyde scheme was one of the most protracted and complex in his charge. Suspended in 1847, resumed in January 1848, its workforce of 4-500 men vigorously excavated the river until reduced to a mere 22 men by the last week of July. Manning was perturbed to let so many men go 'at a time when no work could be otherwise obtained' and tried to manage the upheaval gently, acknowledging that there was 'not a single instance of a breach of the peace or any misconduct on the part of the labourers', most of whom had sunk into exhausted apathy. Two bridges were rebuilt in late 1848 with the tiny remaining force, and works were carried on fitfully.

During 1851 Manning found it 'very difficult to obtain men' for the relatively low wages on offer but managed to dig a channel seventy feet wide from low-water mark on Dundalk Bay to Annagassan Bridge (which was underpinned). Three mill-races were excavated and wrought-iron conduits prepared for each one. A mill-weir, sluices, salmon-pass and wheel-conduit were raised on the Killany tributary.

During 1852 and 1853 when the bulk of the final work was done Manning supervised the construction of more sluices, fixed conduits in masonry, deepened the river channel, piled embankments, built several stone bridges and ten wooden accommodation bridges, in the process clearing much flood debris from the winter-storms of 1852-53 out of the watercourse.

1854/5: Drainage schemes draw to a close

By late 1853 the drainage schemes were coming to a close and Manning was sounding out the jobs market with little result. He limped through 1854 and 1855 on a weakened Board of Works contract which turned into a 'verbal agreement' on drastically lower wages. Though tempted over Christmas 1854 by a lucrative offer of employment on the staff of the East India Company, he decided instead to take the risk of staying in Ireland with his family.

Lord Downshire's estate engineer 1856-68

His patience was rewarded in late 1855 or early 1856 when he won a contract for the completion of a topographical survey of the Downshire estates in County Down for the purpose of accurately 'laying out improvements'. For the next twelve years Manning held the comfortable situation of estate engineer under the fourth Marquis at a salary of £400 per annum until 1865 and £500 per annum thereafter. This involved the performance of a multiplicity of duties in the matters of drainage, river and land improvement, bridges, fencing, road-making and ornamental works. In many of these matters Manning would have been in regular correspondence with the Board of Works as a lending agency.

One of the Board fishery inspectors, William J. Fennell, supplies a vignette of Manning at work in Dundrum, County Down, in May 1858, incidentally ticking him off for neglecting to install a fish-pass on an estate mill-dam: 'I found very extensive works being carried on…a causeway has been made to the Island of Murlough and a wooden bridge, about 200 feet long by 20 broad, under the direction of Mr Manning…a dwelling house on the island…and…cottages for fishermen…(are building and planned)…he has also built a steam-dredge to improve the entrance at the bar and means to extend the quay in the town'.

In the 1860s Manning carried out intensive scientific

Lord Downshire's funeral in Hillsborough, Co. Down (Illustrated London News, National Library of Ireland)

51 St Stephen's Green, Dublin. The present home of the Office of Public Works was formerly the Royal College of Science, where Manning worked on his famous hydrological formula.

work on aspects of rainfall, river volume and water runoff in respect of the mooted use of rivers on the Downshire estates for the water-supply of Belfast. As in most of his work he ventured into new areas of theory and practice and a paper on the subject delivered to the British Institute of Civil Engineers in May 1866 earned him the Telford Gold Medal and a Manby Premium.

1868: Appointed engineer in Board of Works

This industrious idyll came to an end after the death of the fourth Marquis of Downshire in August 1868 and Manning was told in December 1868 that his post as engineer was to finish within nine months. It was fortunate that the Board of Works offered a lifeline that year, as an engineering post fell vacant. Manning was appointed second engineer under his old colleague William Forsyth on 1st October 1869 on a starting salary of £300 per annum.

In this first phase of his second term of office in the Board of Works, the departmental work appears to have been shared equally between the two engineers: Forsyth had little interest in the assertion of rank where everyone was snowed under with urgent contractual work. Forsyth retired exactly one year later and Manning was appointed chief engineer on 1st April 1874 on a fixed salary of £800 per annum. The office duties were extensive while the permanent staff was far too small.

1874-91: Hard work as Chief Engineer

Manning was vested with the care of the five 'Royal' harbours and numerous fishery piers and small havens, the inland navigations, continual inspection of the arterial drainage, monitoring county roads and certain specific public highways, and 'subjects connected with sewage, water supply, mills, graving docks, markets etc'. The day was never long enough: indeed Manning worked out that each year in the 1870s he spent some 84 days out of office travelling and made do with nine or ten days holidays (in his case doubling as sick leave): 'we really get no leave'.

In 1877 (the year it received its Royal Charter) he served as president of the Institution of Civil Engineers of Ireland, having been made full member in 1856 and elected to the council in 1873. Describing himself in March 1884 as primarily a 'marine engineer', some of his most outstanding work between 1874 and 1891 was done on the coast. He designed and constructed some 100 piers and harbours during his tenure, about 30 built under the Relief of Distress Act of 1880 and 61 undertaken under the Sea Fisheries Act of 1883. At his retirement the Board of Commissioners chose particularly to highlight the skill displayed in the Arklow works of 1882 to 1890, 'which presented difficulties from the yielding nature of the foundations and exposed position on the coast of a very exceptional character'.

They were silent about the character of the political and other opposition which Manning had also to confront and turn around. The piers there had been smashed up in storms in the mid-1870s and Manning surveyed the peculiarities of the harbour in 1875, finding it 'different from any other harbour that I know of'. A Bill was eventually passed in 1882 permitting the Board to go ahead with the new piers. Manning determined on the construction of a new pier and a groin against the 'destructive' south-east wind but had to contend for some years with a furious cross-wind of local opinion and political abuse. Kearon, the Arklow harbour commissioner, admitted, however, in February 1890, the excellence of the new works compared to the shambles that had brought 'sheer desperation' to fishing vessels in the 1850s.

Manning's pioneering formula for Open Channel Flow

Given the stresses of office, it is amazing that Manning was able to find leisure in his last years in the Custom House to develop and refine a pioneering formulation for calculating the velocity of flow of water 'in open channels and pipes'. This was the crowning glory of his career. It has been shown by Professor James Dooge that Manning, while living at 4 Ely Place, did most of the work on this equation in the Library of the Royal College of Science at 51 St Stephen's Green, the present home of the Office of Public Works.

The first version of the formula was revealed in a paper delivered at Trinity College, Dublin to the Institution of Civil Engineers in December 1889. Manning pointed out the confusion at the time surrounding even the rough calculation of 'the velocity or surface inclination of water', noting that there was no such thing as true uniform motion in river channels and that 'even to observe and record correctly the physical data required was a matter of extreme difficulty' but that nevertheless something better than a complicated 'empirical formula' or rule-of-thumb method ought still to be possible. And this is what he vouchsafed:

$$V = \left(\frac{1}{n}\right) R^{2/3} S^{1/2}$$

where V is the mean velocity (in metres per second), S the channel slope, R the mean hydraulic radius (in metres) and n the Manning roughness co-efficient. Over the next few years he verified the effectiveness of the formula by checking it against some 413 experimental measurements of open channel flow and 230 measurements of pipe flow, finding that it predicted the correct velocity within a small margin of error in 84% of cases (the dataset was derived from a French series compiled between 1855 and 1865). In a paper given to the Institution in May 1895, Manning confirmed his findings. The formula within a few years passed into the standard literature and it is now the most widely accepted method for the calculation of open channel flow throughout the world. He had established one of the building blocks of the science of hydrology. It was a piece of great brilliance from a largely self-taught engineer.

Retires at 75

Commissions of inquiry in the 1870s and 1880s found him a pungent and well-organised interviewee.

It seems that he had some facility as a cartoonist. He retired from the Board of Works in December 1891 at the age of seventy-five at a time when his wife seems to have begun to suffer from dementia. Two of his sons became surveyors or engineers and his four daughters (none of whom married) were painters and musicians (Mary Ruth Manning, a painter of some distinction, was close to Sarah Purser). The death of his wife and the accidental drowning of his youngest son in Canada in 1894 and the sudden death of a granddaughter at Ely Place in April 1896 understandably wore him down. He died at home in Dublin on 9th December 1897, aged 81, and is buried in Mount Jerome.

Annual reports of the Board of Works, 1846-1855; Robert Manning, 'Presidential address', *Transactions of Institution of Civil Engineers of Ireland* (TICEI), vol.12 (1978); *Report of the Committee of Inquiry into the Public Works, Ireland,* House of Commons 1878 (C.2060) xxiii; Robert Manning, 'On the flow of water in open channels and pipes', *TICEI*, vol.20, 1889; Robert Manning, 'On the flow of water in open channels and pipes', *TICEI*, vol.24, 1895; 'Obituary', *Irish Builder*, 15th December 1897; *The Irish Times*, 17th December 1897; J.C.I Dooge, *Robert Manning (1816-1897)*, Institution of the Civil Engineers of Ireland Centenary Lecture, 6th December 1989; Joseph Robins, *Custom House People*, (Dublin, 1993).

William R. Le Fanu

1816 - 1894

Longest serving Commissioner of Public Works in Ireland 1863-91.
(Courtesy National Library of Ireland)

William Richard Le Fanu was one of the most dynamic and skilled railway engineers in 19th century Ireland and a meticulous and well-balanced administrator. Fascinated by hypnotism and field-sports and possessed of a scintillating sense of humour, his social facility almost matched that of Percy French (1854-1920), his erstwhile subordinate in the engineering department of the Board of Works. Where his beloved brother, the novelist, Sheridan Le Fanu, was reclusive, complex and gloomy, William Le Fanu was convivial and ingenuous, enjoying a wide circle of friends of every political persuasion. He was also the longest-serving commissioner in the history of the Office of Public Works (1863-91). His son, T.P. Le Fanu was junior Commissioner from 1914 to 1925.

Happy Anglo-Irish childhood in Dublin and Limerick

Le Fanu was born on 24th February 1816 in the Royal Hibernian Military School (RHMS) in the Phoenix Park, the third and youngest child of the Very Reverend Thomas Philip Le Fanu (1784-1845), chaplain to the RHMS (1815-26), and Emma Lucretia Dobbin (c.1790-1861), daughter of Dr William Dobbin, rector of St Mary's parish, Dublin city. His sister, Catherine Frances (1813-41), died in her twenties. And his older brother, Sheridan Joseph (1814-73), by the 1840s and 1850s had become established as one of the best Irish Victorian novelists. He remembered his childhood in the Phoenix Park as a paradisian collage of 'rambles…military reviews, sham fights and races' edged with the fearful excitement of duelling on the open pastures near the school. The family was close-knit. In William's case this strengthened an outgoing disposition and a regard for uncomplicated family loyalties (the family servants from the 1820s died in his Dublin home in the 1870s and 1880s). His brother instead brooded on the spiritual confines of kinship and excruciating tensions created by narrow social circulation within the Anglo-Irish minority.

In 1826 the family moved to the parish of Abington, Co. Limerick (20 miles from the city), a good living,

where Le Fanu and his brother were first schooled in Latin and Greek by one John Stinson, an aged and irregular cleric, fond of the bagpipes and fly-fishing, while their father looked after their English and French. This was where Le Fanu acquired his first taste of angling and a lifelong dexterity in tying flies. Nothing much else was taught however, Stinson was sacked and their father took over all the teaching duties. In this country parish Le Fanu encountered faction fights, agrarian outrages and belief in changelings. During the tithe war of 1831 to 1834 relations with the local peasantry soured and Le Fanu at one time narrowly escaped serious injury in a misguided attempt at negotiation with farmers over tithe payments. Fortunately (and ironically), their father secured a post on a commission of inquiry into Irish tithes and the family moved for the greater part of the conflict to Dublin (1832-34).

1839: Apprenticed in Dublin

Le Fanu entered Trinity College Dublin in November 1833, taking six years to graduate BA in May 1839: it seems that 'being on the country list' the brothers were allowed take their time doing exams. In the summer of 1839 Le Fanu was accepted into the Dublin office of John Benjamin MacNeill (1793-1880) the eminent railway engineer and future (somewhat remote) first professor of the TCD school of engineering (1842-1852). It was a hectic office in which to start an apprenticeship and Le Fanu, as one of several assistants (including Matthew Blakiston and the future sculptor, John Jones) was thrown without ceremony in at the deep end: MacNeill had jobs all over England and needed assistants to stand in for him in Ireland. Le Fanu was also called on regularly 'every spring and early summer' to aid MacNeill in London during the fussy legal preliminaries to the enactment of Railway Bills in the House of Commons. His high spirits were little dented by the driving work: in the summer of 1840 he came from a fancy dress ball in a peasant costume into the Dublin office successfully begging MacNeill and his fellow pupils for help getting back to 'my native Tipperary'.

1840: Dublin-Drogheda railway

The Dublin-Drogheda line, the second major railway in Ireland, began construction in October 1840. As the early locomotives were not powerful enough to deal with much of a gradient, lines had to be as nearly level as possible, posing considerable engineering difficulties in rolling countryside but providing exceptional learning opportunities for the young engineer. The line issued from Amiens Street on one of the longest lattice-girder bridges of its type in the world. At Clontarf, Malahide, and Rogerstown, Le Fanu was responsible in 1842 and 1843 for the construction of massive stone-pitched sea embankments spanning soft mud estuaries and inlets. He 'constantly travelled' between Dublin and Drogheda on the obsolescent mail-coach, observing the coachman grow more morose as the works were completed. The line was opened in April 1844 and the embankments held satisfactorily though tested the following winter by 'high tide and storm'.

The Great Southern and Western railway

During the 'railway mania' of 1845 Le Fanu was assigned to the Dublin-Mallow line, the first stage in the Great Southern and Western Railway on its path to Limerick, Cork and Kerry: 'all over the country engineers and surveyors were levelling and surveying'. Though he was elected a member of the Royal Irish Academy in February 1845 and joined the British Institute of Civil Engineers in May 1853, it is curious that he never graced the Irish Institution. Made resident engineer for the MacNeill office on the GS & WR line in January 1846, Le Fanu continued the working relationship forged earlier on the Drogheda line with the renowned contractor, William Dargan (1799-1867). Construction started in early 1846 and the line reached Carlow in August that year. Lines were opened to Portlaoise by June 1847 and to Thurles by March 1848 and to Limerick junction by July that year.

The construction of the railways continued during the extreme distress of the Great Famine. (Illustrated London New).

A narrow gauge system crossing viaduct at Ballydehob, Co. Cork, photo taken in the 1800s during the time of 'railway mania'. (Courtesy National Library of Ireland)

Famine distress

In the acute distress of the period Le Fanu had to deal with much intimidation on the works: three gangers were murdered in 1847. He recalled 'walking along the railway works' near Mallow around March 1849 and witnessing 'dogs fighting and howling…over the bodies of some poor creatures' torn from shallow graves: 'the same night I had to start for London, and next evening saw a carpet spread across the footway to the carriage way, lest the damp should chill the feet or soil the shoes of some fashionable lady. The contrast was a painful one'.

Railway engineer in Cork

Some time around 1848 MacNeill severed his connections with the GS & WR and Le Fanu was appointed consultant engineer to the company. Moving to Rathpeacon House, near the appointed spot for the Cork city goods terminus of the GS & WR, Le Fanu brought the line into Cork in October 1849. Between then and the early 1860s he designed and oversaw the construction of a number of branch lines from the main GS & WR axis. While living in Cork he also revelled in the salmon and trout fishing on the Lee and its tributaries and in snipe shooting on the West Cork and Kerry lands of his aristocratic acquaintances: he calculated in his memoirs that from 1848 to 1892 he had killed an unbelievable 1295 salmon, 2636 sea trout, 65,436 river trout (often little ones from mountain streams) and 602 pike! Late in life he mourned the deterioration of snipe shooting due to extensive land reclamation and drainage (mostly of course by the Board of Works).

Seeing hypnosis or 'electro-biology' for the first time in a London show in 1851, he 'began experimenting on his own account', once memorably convincing a sceptical Isaac Butt at Rathpeacon House of the truth of the hypnotic state by practising on some railway navvies. On behalf of the GS & WR he engineered a branch line from Millstreet to Killarney in 1852-53, a line to Tullamore in 1854, tracks from Ballybrophy to Roscrea in 1857, a line

from Ballingrane to Foynes in 1857-58, one to Athlone in 1858-59, from Mallow to Fermoy between 1857 and 1860 and from Roscrea to Nenagh between 1858 and 1863, apart from the constant supervision and repair of the permanent way laid down since 1846.

Successful private engineering practice

As part of his private practice Le Fanu undertook the engineering of the Tipperary-Clonmel section of the Waterford-Limerick line between 1851 and 1853, crossing the River Suir at Cahir on a wrought-iron box girder bridge 250 feet long. He did the short excursion line from Waterford to Tramore in 1853, and in 1855-56 constructed a standard gauge line from Borris (Carlow) to Ballywilliam (Wexford), carried near the first station by a spectacular limestone viaduct 470 feet long.

During the 1850s he built up 'I may safely say…the largest practice of any man in Ireland at the time', earning some £9000 after tax in 1857. In January that year he married Henrietta Barrington (d.1899), youngest daughter of Sir Matthew Barrington, Crown Solicitor for Munster. They had eight children. From 1861 to 1863 he held a consultancy for Irish Lights. In 1863, 'much pressed…by my friends in the Irish government', Le Fanu took up the offer of junior Commissioner of the Board of Works. As a car-driver suggested to him in 1864, on a trip from Bray to town, though he made less money, 'the situation is more respectable like'.

Duties as junior Commissioner

Between 1863 and 1872 he was accorded the supervision of the various coastguard stations being built on contract that decade: this required considerable travel and inspection. But for most of his career in the Board of Works he remained at his desk in the Custom House dealing principally with the administration of the Public Work Loan Fund, the Irish Reproductive Loan Fund, loans under the Land Improvement Acts and under the Landlord and Tenant Acts of 1870 (amended in 1872), loans for

The Great Southern and Western railway station at Kenmare, Co. Kerry.
(Courtesy National Photographic Archive, Lawrence Collection)

Le Fanu was a frequent and popular guest at the Viceregal Lodge
in Phoenix Park. (Courtesy National Photographic Archive,
Lawrence Collection)

drainage, railway loans, loans for county roads and a multiplicity of other subsidiary loans and forms of assistance or regulation.

As a body of Commissioners John Graham McKerlie and himself were later criticised for failing to hold formal board meetings but much of their practice arose from the practical and good-natured working relationship developed by the pair. As Le Fanu stated in 1878: 'every question that arises, or every question that involves a new principle, or…that I think the chairman would wish to be apprised of, I go into his room and consult him on it before I make any minute…I believe he does the same…in most of the cases of an important character…on many days we have several subjects to bring under his notice'.

Railway loans

In the matter of railway loans he was, of course, supremely conversant with the practical details of proposals coming under consideration: 'we inquire into all the circumstances of the line - as to its state - as to the borrowing powers of the company and everything connected with their financial affairs and with the line and works'. But his business friendships did not seem to incline him unduly towards the endorsement of loans: if anything railway companies found him strict on inquiry - he had a clear idea of the speculative nature of most railways (indeed few lines did well: it was often only the engineers and contractors who profited).

A frequent and popular guest

Le Fanu acted as member of the Board of Control for Lunatic Asylums, attending a weekly meeting in Dublin Castle. He was a frequent and popular guest, in an official and unofficial capacity, at levees and formal evenings in the Viceregal lodge, Phoenix Park.

He saved up funny correspondence for light relief at meetings and for his memoirs. One correspondent memorably asked for a taste of a haunch of venison from the Phoenix Park herd. A small farmer in the 1870s held the balance of a loan for £8 'which he would neither expend nor refund'. After many fruitless endeavours to make him do one or the other, a peremptory letter was sent to him, saying that if he did not within a week repay the amount, the Board's solicitor would be directed to take proceedings at once against him for its recovery. He replied as follows: 'My dear secretary and gentlemen of the honourable Board of Works, asking me to give back £8 is just like asking a beautiful and healthy young lady for a divorce, and she in the utmost love with her husband, as I am with each and every one of ye. I am your sincere friend, James Clarke'.

And there was the, perhaps apocryphal, story of the Tipperary grand jury preparing three resolutions to back up the integrity of the process of loan being initiated at the Board of Works: 'First, that a new courthouse shall be built. Second, that the materials of the old courthouse be used in building the new courthouse. Third, that the old courthouse shall not be taken down till the new court house is finished'.

Lifelong friendships

Many of the stories told in his memoir Seventy Years of Irish Life are genuinely side-splitting. Though light in tone, the comic timing is excellent: nothing is ever funny unless it is well told. As a man of 'courtesy, refinement and superior conversational powers', he developed lifelong friendships with Anthony Trollope, Isaac Butt, Morgan John O'Connell and James O'Connell (Daniel O'Connell's sons), William Thackeray, John Jones, Charles Bianconi, William Dargan, Sheridan Knowles the actor and dramatist and numerous others in engineering, politics and the arts. He retired from the Board of Works in 1891 and died on 8th September 1894 at his residence in Summerhill, Enniskerry, County Wicklow. He was buried in the local churchyard.

Report of the Committee of Inquiry into Public Works, Ireland, House of Commons, 1878 (C.2060) xxiii; W.R. Le Fanu, *Seventy years of Irish Life* (London, 1893); *Irish Times,* 10 Sept 1894; *Freeman's Journal,* 11-12 Sept 1894; T.P. Le Fanu, *Memoir of the Le Fanu family* (Dublin, 1924); K.A. Murray and D.B. McNeill, *The Great Southern and Western Railway* (Dublin, 1976); W.J. McCormack, *Sheridan Le Fanu* (Oxford, 1980); J.W.P Rowledge, *A Regional History of Railways, vol. xvi: Ireland* (Trowbridge, 1995); Stephen Johnson, *Johnson's Atlas and Gazetteer of the Railways of Ireland* (Leicester, 1997); R.C. Cox and M.H. Gould, *Civil Engineering Heritage, Ireland* (London, 1998); Edward Patterson, *The Great Northern Railway (Ireland)* (Usk, 2003); R.C. Cox, 'William Le Fanu', in P.S.M. Cross-Rudkin, (ed.), *A Biographical Dictionary of Civil Engineers in Great Britain and Ireland, volume 2: 1831-1890* (forthcoming, London 2007); Stephanie P. Jones, 'William Richard Le Fanu', in *Royal Irish Academy's Dictionary of Irish Biography,* (forthcoming).

Harold G. Leask

1882 - 1964

OPW 1908-49; Inspector of National Monuments.
(Courtesy Royal Society of Antiquaries of Ireland)

Harold George Leask was eclectic in his enthusiasms and range of skills; one of his foremost attributes was the way he communicated, in his writings and talks, a zestful interest and reverence for the remains of past cultures in Ireland. The popular nationalism of the early 20th century was mainly concerned, for all the wrong reasons, with the splendours of the 'Celtic' and early Christian built heritage. As Inspector of National Monuments in the 1920s, he bridged the gap between 19th century assumptions about the care of monuments and the world of the modern discipline. His published work strongly but unobtrusively brought into the popular consciousness a wider interest and respect for the complexities of medieval culture.

Leask's drawing of the Winged Harp from the south front portico of the Custom House. (Courtesy Irish Architectural Archive)

Promising apprentice draughtsman in Dublin

He was born on 7th November 1882 at Ashfield Terrace, Harold's Cross, Dublin, only son of Robert Leask, architect and civil engineer. In 1898, aged 16, he was made apprentice draughtsman and surveyor in his father's office at 37 College Green. The following year he was elected member to the Architectural Association of Ireland. Receiving his articles in 1903, he gained experience for a spell in a Dublin iron-foundry while continuing with his studies. Each year between 1904 and 1906 he produced prize-winning design work at the Association. After a period in a Waterford drawing office circa 1904-05 he was employed for two years in the Suffolk Street office of the noted architect George Patrick Sheridan. Returning as senior assistant around 1907 to the Leask office round the corner he became active at committee level in the Architectural Association, winning the vice-president's prize in 1908.

Appointed surveyor in OPW

It appears that he was taken on in the post of temporary assistant surveyor at the Office of Public Works in late 1908 when he was involved in planning minor works of improvement in the Dundrum Criminal Lunatic

Asylum. Taking first place in the Civil Service Commission examinations for the OPW in September 1909, he was appointed permanent assistant surveyor (grade II) and in 1910 he moved briefly to Board offices in Dundalk.

Between 1910 and 1914 Leask, in collaboration with his fellow-assistant M.J. Burke, and under the direction of the Principal Architect, Andrew Robinson, turned out designs (among other things) for Tullamore Post Office (1909), Wexford Custom House (1910), Castlerea Post Office (1911), the Supper Room in Dublin Castle (1911), a wireless telegraph station (and torpedo-instructor's house) at Bunbeg, Co Donegal (1911), Roscommon and Tuam Post Offices (both in September 1912), Pearse Street D.M.P. barracks (1912) and the Labour Exchange in Lord Edward Street (1914). It is not always easy to discern whether these works owed their design essentials to his hand or to the hand of a senior architect.

First work in architectural history

In 1913 Leask published his first study in Irish architectural history, a note in the Journal of the Royal Society of Antiquaries on Old Bawn House, County Dublin. It is likely that he had been introduced to architectural heritage by his father, who had an enthusiasm for the buildings of Georgian Dublin and supported the Georgian Society in the early 1900s. Some of Leask's first sketches appeared in the massive pioneering volumes on Irish Georgian architecture brought out between 1905 and 1914: these are identifiably in his style but still lack the confidence of his mature draughtsmanship. Though he became deeply active in the Royal Society of Antiquaries between being elected member in 1910 and receiving the award of Fellowship of the Society in 1920, and clearly extended his antiquarian erudition and his familiarity with medieval and earlier architectural remains, he published little, compared to his enormous later output: in his first fifteen years in the Office of Public Works he was author of only three articles.

1923: Inspector of National Monuments

It is likely that he was accorded some responsibilities in respect of monuments in state care at this period: he drew up the relevant section for the 1916 Annual Report (which was not published due to war-cutbacks). Appointed part-time Inspector of National Monuments in October 1923, Leask lent a hand also in the major reconstruction works going on in Dublin that decade including the Custom House, and in particular enhancing elements of the interior design in the G.P.O. Between 1923 and 1930 Leask was the only permanent member of staff in National Monuments. There were also usually three or four clerks of works on temporary contract and, as occasion demanded, labourers were hired on site for weeks or months at a time. During this period, work (on meagre funds) was undertaken annually on about 20 sites, mostly ecclesiastical structures.

A safe pair of hands

There was some uncertainty as to how the care of monuments was going to evolve in the Irish Free State, and there were sensitive issues underlying the recognition and care of field antiquities. It was widely assumed that only 'nations' were entitled to political independence. And it was a common, vaguely articulated sentiment that the existence of nationhood was demonstrated by long-standing cultural unity within a given 'national' territory. Opening up to view the diverse and often contending elements of population and culture that actually contributed to the formation of Irish society, and which tended to be concealed or explained away in the simpler forms of political debate, might open up the kind of insecurities that were typical of most emerging nation-states. As a result, some monuments might look less deserving of state attention than others. In such circumstances Leask was a very safe pair of hands, avoiding polemic or controversy.

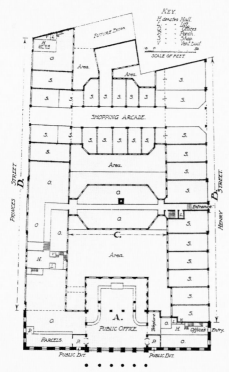

General Post Office, O'Connell Street, Dublin. Ground floor plan, as rebuilt 1924-29

The interior of the General Post Office after reconstruction in 1926.

Conservation or restoration?

National Monuments operated in the 1920s within the parameters of the Ancient Monuments Protection (Ireland) Act of 1892, as modified by the Local Government Act of 1898. The emphasis in the conservation policy was on the need strictly to 'preserve' monuments rather than to risk dubious rebuilding or restoration work. This implied economy and restraint in pointing or reworking masonry, so that essential efforts to consolidate parts of a ruin at risk of collapse were made plain to later visitors: old and new work had to remain visibly distinct. Heavier attempts at restoration were anathema. Again, this was not merely an issue of aesthetics: the original stock of monuments in state care had been transferred from the ownership of the Church of Ireland in 1869 at a time when there was Catholic nationalist muttering that the older sites ought to have been vested in the Roman Catholic church and re-consecrated for ritual use. There was widespread professional agreement that the legislation needed updating but it took several years for this to come to pass.

1930 Act brings improvements

The National Monuments Act of 1930 took most of its shape from a draft bill proposed in 1925 by a joint committee of the RSAI and the RIAI to which Leask contributed a good deal. The Act had several new features bearing on Leask's activities. First, the destructive concept of a 'date-bar' in the designation of monuments was taken out of the legislation; uninhabited buildings of almost any age theoretically could now be listed. The misleading distinction previously made between 'ancient' and 'national' monuments was scrapped. The legal forms under which monuments were taken into state care were better defined. Local authorities were allotted some financial and other responsibilities for the care of monuments. The OPW was confirmed as executive authority under the Minister of Finance for the provisions of the Act. And the Inspector of National Monuments, as agent of the OPW, was placed in full-time responsibility.

Importantly, the OPW now regulated the issue of licences for archaeological excavation and this was to be a large part of Leask's expanding brief.

As Inspector of National Monuments, Leask would be required to advise the Commissioners on 'all monuments, their nature, character, interest and condition the steps to be taken for their protection, repair and maintenance and directs all necessary work'. The stress remained on the 'preservation or protection' of monuments. Leask was temperamentally inclined to a cautious minimalism and had not the money in any case to attempt novelties of restoration. In a sense the whole divide was a matter of spirit and interpretation. He owned to a romantic preference for the 'striking and picturesque' atmosphere of roofless buildings. In practice some clerks of works were given space to do more than perhaps Leask would have done on his own.

Monasterboice High Cross, Co Louth. As Inspector of National Monuments, Leask undertook intensive work between 1923 and 1949. (Courtesy Department of the Environment, Heritage and Local Government)

Increased monument repair work in 1930s and 40s

It is not yet clear if expenditure fluctuated much in the 1930s and 1940s. But the number of sites under ongoing repair rose appreciably in the 1930s to 25 or 30 each year. Between 1923 and 1949, during his entire term in office, repairs were carried out some 480 times on 268 separate monuments. Of this array of monuments, 56 (or 21%) were castles and 31 (or 11%) were pre-Christian sites. The rest (181) were early Christian or medieval abbeys, churches, high crosses or oratories. Some 161 sites (60%) were dealt with just once in his tenure and 44 (16%) were visited over three to nine seasons apiece.

The most intensive work was undertaken at Monasterboice, the Rock of Cashel, Mellifont Abbey, Glendalough, Holy Cross Abbey and Newgrange. The repair techniques (especially the use of buttresses and concrete insertions and vaults) can look somewhat intrusive and crude to contemporary taste but had the great merit of being simple and undisguised.

Punchestown Long Stone

Work undertaken at the Punchestown Long Stone in Kildare usefully illustrates what 'minor' repairs to a monument might have meant. In late 1931 the stone tumbled without breaking. The owner of the lands vested it in the Commissioners of Public Works and Leask surveyed the stone and its setting and made a small excavation at the base, finding a stone cist formed at one side of a stone socket. Then in July 1934 'the stone was re-erected, with the aid of a shear-legs, a winch and pulley blocks, on a new concrete foundation slab upon which a concrete socket was formed' taking care that the monolith stood at the same height above the surface as before the fall. Though Leask was not formally trained as an archaeologist, his methodologies were rigorous and up-to-date.

The Casino

The salvage of the Casino in Marino, Dublin was one of the more lavish and unusual projects which Leask undertook. This approached more nearly to a work of restoration than Leask ever attempted in National Monuments, but this was done on the understanding that the building was quite different in type from ruined castles and chapels. At a total cost of about £1500 Leask and his clerk of works, over four years, from 1932 to 1935, made the interior presentable by 'covering up raw surfaces and healing obvious wounds without detracting from the value of the original work'. The rotting roof timbers were replaced with a new light steel and timber roof, flooring and timber in the state room was also replaced, cornices in the saloon were restored and dry rot was treated. Unfortunately these works were not entirely successful but the building was saved for later, more intensive works of restoration.

Leask deepened public awareness

Leask gave more scope to clerks of works than his successor, Percy le Clerc, who became assistant inspector

Punchestown Long Stone, Co Kildare. In July 1934 the stone was re-erected with winch and pulley. (Courtesy Department of the Environment, Heritage and Local Government)

Lord Charlemont's Casino at Marino, Dublin. Leask salvaged this unusual building in 1932-35.(Courtesy Department of the Environment, Heritage and Local Government)

around 1945. He was consistently sympathetic and fair-minded towards tradesmen suffering poor work conditions on terms of little security. He encouraged some of them to take an investigative interest in the monuments and credited their assistance in his articles. Given that his work was so inadequately financed, perhaps one of the most positive achievements open to Leask was to deepen public awareness and understanding through his writings, many of which arose directly out of his conservation work.

Important articles, books and lectures

The big complaint against most professionals in the field of archaeology is that too little work is published. This was not the case with Leask. He turned out 70 essays and notes from 1913 to 1961 and two major studies, a one-volume handbook on Irish Castles (1941) and a three-volume work on Irish Churches and Monastic Buildings (1955-60). This was supplemented by numerous lectures and talks given on tours organised by the Royal Society of the Antiquaries of Ireland and other bodies. Of all 70 articles, most were penned between 1930 and 1946. About half of the articles were on the theme of churches and abbeys (medieval and early Christian) and about a fifth discussed aspects of castles in Ireland. Nearly all of them were adorned by his engaging drawings.

Leask tended to concentrate on architectural questions raised by the structures and touched very little on wider cultural or social issues. The writing is bright and readable, never pedantic or involved. And one of its peculiar qualities is that Leask was able to convey a tangible sense of the buildings under discussion, probably because he had seen and touched and lived with nearly every monument. His manuscript studies only backed up his field observations, which is as it should be.

The sketches create an empathic connection that would have been lacking had photographs only been used in the books and articles. There is a serene and timeless feel to the books, in particular, which probably means they could never be superseded by more academic works.

If there was any public resistance, due to philistinism or nationalism or a mixture of both, to an appreciation of the value of such structures, this was the best way to undermine it, subtly and gracefully, with the minimum of noise.

Active in retirement

Leask retired from National Monuments in 1949 and with the support of his wife, the distinguished historian, Ada Longfield (1898-1987) whom he had married in 1940, he worked strenuously on the three Irish Church volumes. These treated the buildings more substantially than he had time to do in the case of the work on Irish Castles. Another work, on 17th century fortified houses, was unfortunately not completed at the time of his death (there may perhaps have been enough done to make it worth editing). He spoke on field excursions almost into his eighties, dying after a year or two of ill-health on 25th September 1964.

H.G. Leask, 'The Long Stone, Punchestown, Co. Kildare', *Journal of the Royal Society of Antiquaries of Ireland* (JRSAI), vol.67 (1937), pp.250-52; Harold Leask, *Irish Castles and Castellated Houses* (Dundalk, 1941); Harold Leask, *Irish Churches and Monastic Buildings: the first phases and the Romanesque* (Dundalk, 1955); A.T. Lucas, 'Appreciation of Harold G. Leask', *JRSAI*, vol.96 (1966), pp.1-6; T.A. Dunphy, 'Harold Leask, former Inspector of National Monuments', *Oibre*, vol.7, (1969); Anne Carey, 'Harold G. Leask: aspects of his work as Inspector of National Monuments', *JRSAI*, vol.133 (2003), pp.24-35; Anne Carey, 'Dr Harold G. Leask and the conservation of national monuments in the Irish Free State and Eire, 1923-1949', unpublished thesis for Master of Urban and Building Conservation degree, University College, Dublin (February 2004); Ann Martha Rowan, *Biographical Index of Irish architects*, Irish Architectural Archive (1998-2006).

T.J. Byrne

1876 - 1939

Principal Architect OPW 1923-39.
(*Irish Builder* 1923. Photo courtesy Irish Architectural Archive)

Thomas Joseph Byrne's major achievement was the sensitive and often ingenious reconstruction of several of the great buildings of the capital. He won eminence in professional administration and introduced pioneering concepts of design to housing the poor.

Articled in London

He was born 15th November 1876 in Kingston-on-Thames, Surrey, England, elder of two sons, to the Irish-born Richard Byrne (died c.1878), of the Royal Irish Fusiliers and Harriet (Knight) Byrne. After a local primary and secondary education he was articled to Edward Carter ARIBA of London, working and studying under his wing for three years. In 1895 he parted amicably for a time from Carter to move to the office of Anthony Scott (1845/6-1919) of Drogheda and Navan (later Dublin), his uncle by marriage. This was perhaps his formative professional experience.

In his uncle office in Ireland

Scott, who was very friendly with D P Moran, the Irish nationalist radical journalist, was a kind but taciturn and driven individual who expected much the same qualities of his staff. Having won 'wide and varied experience' of construction, design and restoration work during his tenure at the Board of Works in the 1870s and 1880s, principally as clerk of works to Thomas Newenham Deane, Scott found his business thrived mostly on commissions from the Catholic Church and on cottage schemes for the poor assigned by the Meath and Dublin County Councils. Byrne worked round the clock on contracts and competition entries, while squeezing in nocturnal studies for the Royal Institute of British Architects (RIBA) examinations.

Arts and Crafts principles in Byrne's designs

Byrne took his bearings within the architectural landscape of the day primarily from the Arts and Crafts movement in its later flowering, with its emphasis on

Clondalkin Public Library, Dublin. A 'forceful' example of the Carnegie Libraries TJ Byrne designed on Arts & Crafts principles, 1910-12.

The General Post Office. Proposed new façade to Henry Street by T J Byrne. (*Irish Builder*, July 1924)

durable craftsmanship and the use of local materials. His uncle believed in the reinvigoration of native stonework design in the tradition of medieval and older Irish ecclesiastical architecture and his slightly older first cousin (and colleague, in Drogheda and London), William A Scott (1871-1921), turned out to be perhaps the foremost exponent of the movement in Ireland.

Qualifies ARIBA

Transferring back to the office of Edward Carter in 1898, Byrne came first in the RIBA intermediate exams that year. Around May 1899 Byrne got through his final exams and qualified for his RIBA associateship. The following year he was appointed assistant architect in the progressive Architectural Department of London County Council. In this environment he assimilated some of the enlightened values of early welfare and 'garden city' enthusiasts.

Social concerns in design

Designing fire stations for the council, he developed an 'extensive knowledge' of the demands of structural engineering in steel. Set the task of remodelling the late-19th century Rowton hostels (subsidised short-term accommodation for the working city poor), Byrne was encouraged first to board for some time in one of them in order to acquire 'intimate acquaintance with the working system' of these places and the practical 'needs and daily life' of the residents.

Returns to Ireland 1901

Returning to Ireland in 1901, he was made architect and senior clerk of works to the South Dublin Rural District Council (formed under Act in 1898). This was his principal source of income (he did little private work) from then until 1919. On the strength of this job he was enabled in 1901 to marry Mary Ellen (May) Scott, eldest daughter of Anthony Scott. The couple had two sons (both became engineers) and two daughters (one of

whom lectured in Romance Languages in University College, Cork).

Libraries and housing schemes

In 1910-12 Byrne produced pleasing Carnegie libraries in Clondalkin, Ballyboden and Rathfarnham, explicitly on Arts and Crafts principles and indulging some uncharacteristically playful impulses in their fenestration and ornament. The Clondalkin library has been regarded as a forceful example of the type.

His work entailed primarily the development of labourers' housing in the villages of the south County (many funded through Board of Works loans). These were designed by Byrne to cater for the social needs of labouring families to a greater extent than had been the norm. The dwellings were made as spacious and well-proportioned as possible within rather strict budgetary requirements and were accorded sizeable garden plots. On the contemporary issue whether there was any need to include 'parlours' in these houses Byrne took the view that 'at least 90 per cent of the houses in any scheme' ought to be allowed such a comfort, reflecting a humane insight into some of the indignities of class difference. Bearing in mind that such housing tended usually to be placed in low-lying or inferior locations, Byrne was also unusual in recognising that 'aspect was at least as essential in a labourer's cottage as in a more ostentatious dwelling'.

By the end of the First World War he was the acknowledged Irish authority in this field of housing, nominated in 1918 by the Royal Institute of the Architects of Ireland as one of three assessors to a government-sponsored competition for housing schemes. Between 1919 and 1923 Byrne worked as senior housing inspector to the Local Government Board.

1923: Principal Architect, OPW

In April 1923 he was appointed Principal Architect in the Office of Public Works, plunging directly into the vast problems of reconstruction facing the public offices in

The Four Courts after bombardment in 1922. (Courtesy Irish Architectural Archive)

The Four Courts, Dublin

Dublin. Though the façade of the General Post Office on O'Connell St had survived fairly intact, the interior of the building had been destroyed by continuous bombardment during Easter Week 1916.

The Custom House had been torched by the Dublin Brigade of the IRA on 25th May 1921, burning for five days at extreme temperatures which turned the interior into a tangled mass of ironwork and rubble; in this case the river façade was the least harmed of the structural elevations.

The Four Courts had gone up in smoke on 29th June 1922 at the start of the Civil War. In the political circumstances at the time, though in each case the government considered razing the remains of these buildings and putting up brand-new offices in their stead, it proved (to our benefit) more attractive to restore the calming glories of Georgian and early Victorian architecture to the capital. It may also have served to answer gibes and criticisms from Westminster as to the competence of the fledgling state.

As the sites were cleared (a hazardous process in itself), Byrne thought out designs for appropriate restoration with improvements in the interior arrangements of each building.

Post 1923 reconstruction of GPO, Custom House and Four Courts

The GPO was refurbished between 1925 and 1932 with assistance from J.M. Fairweather and Harold Leask of the OPW. Having first undertaken the Henry Street elevation where room for 13 shops was allotted on the ground floor, Byrne supervised the creation of an arcade running into Prince's Street. The public office was enlarged somewhat and handsomely reappointed to modern specifications.

The exterior of the Custom House was repaired and rebuilt where necessary in a form as close as possible to the original work while the office accommodation was rationalised greatly. The new brightly-lit offices were supported by modernised facilities installed and completed by 1930.

At the Four Courts the 'lively work' of salvage and clearance of debris and 'intractable vitreous concrete' began in 1923. After some hesitation, when consideration was given to establishing accommodation for the Oireachtas on the site, it was determined to recreate the external layout in granite and Portland stone. The main walls were braced by steel framing carrying reinforced concrete floors, 'reconciling the old plan lines with the requirements of modern public buildings and modern office practice'. In consultation with a Law Courts Committee set up for the purpose, Byrne simplified the 'gloomy labyrinth' of the original interior design: he may have been helped by the fact that most 'found it difficult to remember what the building inside was like before'.

Having touched up, replaced or repositioned the 24 Corinthian columns belonging to the peristyle of the majestic copper dome, the work of reconstructing the cupola and drum was a matter of great precision and nerve. The reinforced concrete shell was put in place by a team of 20 men working almost without interruption for 30 hours. This was the first major work of such a kind accomplished in England or Ireland. The reconstruction of the Four Courts between 1925 and 1932, as of the GPO and the Custom House, successfully married advances in modern technology and modern taste in office layout to respect for the grandeur of the original works.

Islandbridge War Memorial

Though Byrne was absorbed for much of the 1930s in work as executant architect on the War Memorial Garden at Islandbridge (designed by Lutyens) which took considerable man-management due to the decision to do much of the work by hand as a means of relieving problems of unemployment during the Depression, the works of the 1920s were his most important contribution to Irish architecture.

The north front central portico of the Custom House. The building was torched in 1921 and burned for 5 days.(Irish Architectural Archive)

The Custom House.

Professional administration

During the 1920s and 1930s he was also very active in the domain of professional administration, serving frequently on the council of the Royal Institute of the Architects of Ireland (1923, 1929, 1930, 1933, 1935, 1938, 1939) and accepting election to presidency of the Irish Architectural Association (IAA) in 1923-24. He was also a member of the Institution of Civil Engineers of Ireland (ICEI) from 1917 and was raised to the council during 1930-31.

Using the platform of the IAA Presidency in 1923-24, Byrne voiced ideals of simple patriotic austerity in keeping with the tone of the new state: 'there is no more room for slackers in our ranks, than there is in any other association or community in the Saorstat. We want workers!…for most human ills there is no remedy so sovereign as work…the real prosperity and content which awaits this land of ours when all our people work are beyond telling'. Though Byrne had a practical sympathy for the needs of the labouring class this did not extend to tolerance for rights of industrial dispute: 'is not the present universal unrest largely due to the prevalence of the opinion that the less work one does the better'.

He was probably not the easiest taskmaster. His articulated views in the 1920s also confirmed an underlying bias towards the values of the Arts and Crafts movement, deprecating any erosion of craft skills under the impact of mechanisation. Reticent and undemonstrative in personality, he was described in May 1923 as having 'the silver hair' of a man in his sixties along with 'the freshness of complexion', incisive judgement and self-possession of a man in his thirties (perhaps not every man). He figures as a gentle but remote childhood presence in the reminiscences of his eldest daughter: she hears reports of what he has been doing rather than sees him much around the house. He suffered from ill-health in the later 1930s and died at his home in 11 Terenure Road East on 27th January 1939, two years before he was due to retire from the OPW. If architecture can communicate an emotional tone to the daily life of citizen or subject, his work did something to stabilise the ethos of state.

T.J. Byrne, 'Rural housing', *Irish Builder*, 15th January 1916, pp.26-28; Oculus, 'May I come in?', *Irish Builder and Engineer*, 19th May 1923, pp.373-74; 'Inaugural address of President of AAI', *Irish Builder and Engineer*, 1st December 1923, p.917; T.J. Byrne, 'Housing in the Saorstat', *Irish Builder and Engineer*, 31st May 1924, p.477; Ethna Bee Cee, *Ethna Mary Twice* (New York, 1989); Frederick O'Dwyer, 'The architecture of the Board of Public Works, 1831-1923', in John Regan and Ciaran O'Connor (eds.) *Public Works; the architecture of the Office of Public Works, 1831-1987* (Dublin, 1987), pp.10-32; Jeremy Williams, *A Companion Guide to Architecture in Ireland, 1837-1921* (Dublin, 1994); Nicola Gordon Bowe and Elizabeth Cumming, *The Arts and Crafts Movements in Dublin and Edinburgh, 1885-1925* (Dublin, 1998); Ann Martha Rowan, *Biographical Index of Irish architects*, Irish Architectural Archive (1998-2006).

The War Memorial Garden at Islandbridge (Courtesy Department of the Environment, Heritage and Local Government).

Raymond McGrath

1903 - 1977

OPW 1940-68. Principal Architect 1948-68. (Photograph by
Dorothy Wilding. Courtesy Irish Architectural Archive)

Thoughts of Raymond McGrath's career as Principal Architect in the Office of Public Works are naturally informed by the idea that he was able to achieve less than he might have done. The depressed Irish economy and discouraging political culture during the 1940s and 1950s could not provide for the great public buildings that would have given scope for his imaginative brilliance and his sensual understanding of materials. His intricate carpet designs, however, and his pristine architectural drawings, paintings and writings communicate a fulfilment of personal presence that remains uplifting. There was an architectural lucidity to his work, in every area of design and writing, that opened up horizons for younger generations in the profession.

Finella - McGrath's 'small but pioneering marvel'. (Courtesy Donal O'Donovan)

Happy Australian childhood

Raymond McGrath was born in Gladesville (near Sydney), New South Wales (Australia) on 7th March 1903, the second of two surviving children, to Herbert McGrath (1876-1963), hospital administrator and Edith Sorrell (d.1946). His grandfather, James McGrath, from a small tenant holding in Carlow, left Ireland in the 1860s, reaching Australia with a small family in 1882. His maternal grandmother, Margaret Bell, was born in Australia of Irish parents in the 1850s. The household lived close enough to the bush for McGrath to grow up knowing his way around raw nature. He and his sister Eileen (born 1907, later a well-known sculptor) were stimulated by a high-minded, individualistic domestic atmosphere.

Studies architecture in Sydney

Showing a real artistic ability by the time he was in his mid-teens, he later went to Sydney University on scholarship in 1921, intending a career in journalism. On the shrewd advice of his English professor, however, he soon switched to architecture. McGrath later argued that the finest public architecture would not re-emerge until 'the powers of the architect and the engineer are

Interior of Finella - 'Clear space and delicate colouring by night and day'. (Courtesy Donal O'Donovan)

greatly united again'. His degree thesis in 1926 was on the transplantation of Chinese architecture to Japan, and further, to its possible significance in modern building design.

A gifted artist

The gifts he had to bring to architecture were impressive. His etchings, linocuts and wood engravings were superbly accomplished in his early twenties: numbers were exhibited and some regarded as among the best of their time. In 1924 he privately published an appealing volume of his poetry with magical woodcuts, 'The seven songs of Meadow Lane'.

Meets Forbes and Frost at Cambridge

Taking first place and first class honours in 1926, McGrath was awarded a three-year travelling fellowship for post-graduate study in Europe. He sailed for London that year, never coming back to Australia.

As a post-graduate student in Cambridge in January 1927, he met the inspirational Mansfield Forbes (1889-1935), who brought him several important commissions in the late 1920s and 1930s, and introduced him to numbers of the leading architects and architectural writers in England, in most cases forming strong and lasting friendships. At Cambridge he met A.C. Frost (d.1963, later his brother-in-law) with whom he was to collaborate. By mid-1927 he was writing articles and reviews and building up a confident appraisal of the good in modern architecture, which was then quite avant-garde in England. Even in the late 1920s he was thinking of opera houses and concert halls - theatre architecture was the subject of his proposed thesis.

1928-29: Finella

In 1928-29 he was 'side-tracked' by Forbes into the creation of a small but pioneering marvel of interior design at 'Finella', a mid-19th century Cambridge house, experimenting there with novel materials (often forms of glass), decorative inlays and uncluttered spaces.

Bursting with ideas, McGrath 'gave the house a feeling of clear space and delicate colouring by night and by day'. Though perhaps more of its time than at first appeared, it became instantly celebrated as a sign of the future and made his name at 26. The most illustrious of contemporary writers, architects and designers found it thrilling.

Creates stylish London interiors

McGrath also met and became engaged to Mary Crozier (b.1908) an American student, while the house was being finished. They were married in June 1930 and lived for some time in Finella. In late 1930, on the strength of his proven finesse, he became 'decoration consultant' on the design of the broadcasting studios in the new BBC headquarters on Oxford Street. In rented offices nearby he ran a substantial practice there, later moving to Conduit Street. The flair and modernity of his London interiors were noted, and the hard-working McGrath was given work on the BBC Manchester studios.

Other intriguing commissions he undertook were for alloyed aircraft furniture, book designs, modernist lamps, roof landing strips, showrooms, museum exhibitions and an aborted project for flats in Knightsbridge, which showed forward-looking ideas on the configuration of apartments.

His interiors for the fashionable Embassy Club (1932) and Fischer's Club (1933) were much praised. Employing a Basic English vocabulary as an exercise in restraint, in 1933 he wrote Twentieth Century Houses, a beautiful study of some 129 examples, half of which were from England and Germany.

1935-36: St. Ann's Hill

Though he included three examples of his own work in the book, it was his next major commission for a modern domestic house at St Ann's Hill, Chertsey (done in 1935-36), that showed his thinking being put into action.

Described as 'the most surprising, daring and satisfying' of the modern English houses of the 1930s, it was naturally built, in cylindrical form, of reinforced concrete, set in a garden designed by Christopher Tunnard. McGrath's own description can't be beaten: 'like a big cheese, with a slice cut for the sunlight to enter the whole house'. It characteristically tried out a new type of faceted glass in one of the doors.

1937: Writes 'Glass in Architecture and Design'

In 1937 McGrath (aided by A.C. Frost) wrote the imposing Glass in Architecture and Design, incorporating erudition with his practical experience. Reprinted in a second edition in 1961, it was advanced in the way it continuously integrated scientific analysis with aesthetic and humane insight. There are few technical books like it.

During 1938 and 1939 property investment was affected by fears of war and commissions failed financially. More devastating still, in 1938 and 1939 his wife began to suffer from manic-depressive illness (they now had two young children, a boy and a girl). In 1939 McGrath secured work as a war artist, turning out delicate studies of aircraft under construction.

1940: Senior Architect in OPW

He was hugely relieved to be offered a post as senior architect in the Office of Public Works later that year. The family moved to Dublin in May 1940 when he began work at 51/52 St Stephen's Green. The period represented a watershed in his personal and professional lives.

It is said that during the 1930s he had stepped back from the vanguard of modernist British architecture and design. It is not easy to discern a clear point of transition, however, perhaps because he published much less after 1940 and revealed less of himself. Glass in Architecture showed greater literary maturity and more profound historical grasp than the text of Twentieth Century Houses (good as that is) but does not suggest that he had lost faith in the principles of modernism. If glass, which inspired

St Ann's Hill – 'like a big cheese with a slice cut for the sunlight to enter the whole house'. (Courtesy Donal O'Donovan)

The Lafranchini Corridor in Aras an Uachtarain.

The State Reception Room in Áras an Uachtaráin. McGrath designed the distinctive carpets, hand-woven in Donegal.

The Cenotaph on Leinster Lawn.

him so greatly, is itself one of the talismanic materials of modernism, it is suggestive that McGrath did not work again in that medium.

The Irish architectural scene in the 1940s

Though it is true that the Irish architectural scene had less progressive stimulus than elsewhere in Europe (McGrath developed an uneasy relationship, at best, with Michael Scott) it was also true that Desmond Fitzgerald and the OPW had embarked in 1940 on the terminal building at Dublin Airport, which was as good (in modernist terms) as anything being done in Britain. Even if the sort of state commissions coming his way from the early 1940s necessitated a marriage of the traditional and the progressive, there is still some mystery as to why the strong modernist tone of the 1930s work became diluted.

Refurbishment of Áras an Uachtaráin

One of his first assignments was the refurbishment of Áras an Uachtaráin (presidential residence from 1938), presenting him immediately with the paradox of having to renew old forms while finding an architectural expression for a new national identity. Opening up the internal space in the building, by the creation of a long State Corridor, lit by skylights and adorned by Lafranchini panels salvaged from Riverstown House, and culminating in a spiral staircase, satisfactorily made the house feel more receptive 'to the nation'.

The question of private practice

As one of the natural ways an architect might get to know Ireland, McGrath studied Irish Georgian architecture thoroughly during the early 1940s, publishing a warm illustrated essay on the streets and buildings of Dublin in The Bell in 1942 - plans to make a book out of an extended version of the piece did not come to fruition. Supported strongly by J.M. Fairweather, principal architect of the OPW, he applied in late 1943 for the post of Professor of Architecture in University College Dublin but did not get the job. State investment in public architecture was scanty at this time, and McGrath argued in 1943 and 1948 for the right to private practice (in his own time of course) as a creative outlet for his powers. From the 1830s to the 1950s the matter of access to private practice in architecture (and in engineering) recurred as a bone of contention within the OPW (as it did in the UK Ministry of Works).

Though the OPW granted the right to industrial work in 1943, McGrath did not exploit the opportunity greatly during his term of office: in the late 1940s he did a little work for some of the centre city hotels and restaurants and in 1953-54 he was called upon to enhance the passenger facilities at Shannon Airport. Criticism of the McGrath proposal of 1945 for a Davis memorial in St Stephen's Green was unfair: the drawings actually suggest a monument resembling in style some of the Lutyens works of this kind (it was undoubtedly too big for the park).

Plans for a National Concert Hall

The first labour pains of the future National Concert Hall were experienced in 1946 when a ministerial committee sounded out plans to convert the Rotunda for some £350,000. McGrath toured Scandinavian, Dutch and Belgian concert halls later that year to check out the latest acoustic and design schemes but the idea was shelved under the Coalition government of 1948-1951, only springing briefly to life in the first months of the returning Fianna Fáil administration. Perhaps the Rotunda scheme might have brought out the best of McGrath's designs for this long-running project.

He was made assistant principal architect in January 1948, three months before Fairweather retired; in May 1948 he became principal architect at a starting salary of £1275 per annum (this had risen to c£1700 by 1951).

Dublin Castle Civil Service offices

Between 1947 and 1949 McGrath conceived a stately curvilinear design (with a traditional 'Georgian' façade)

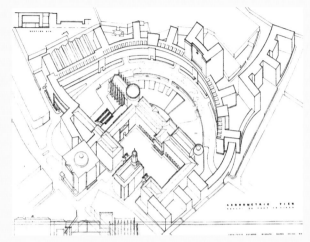

McGrath's plans for new Civil Service Offices in the Lower Yard of Dublin Castle (1947-49).

McGrath's sketches for the proposed CIvil Service Offices in Dublin Castle although blurred by time, show an impressive neo-classical form that would have done well.

for new Civil Service offices in the lower yard of Dublin Castle. The architectural sketches (with small figures leaning into the wind) show an extremely impressive neo-classical form that would probably have done well in practice (it would surely have succeeded better than the Revenue offices erected in 1969-71). Unfortunately this scheme was aborted, for financial reasons, under the Coalition government. The Cenotaph on Leinster Lawn, dedicated in 1950 to the patriotic 'Treatyites', Collins, Griffith and O'Higgins, was a kind of obelisk moved by an impulse towards abstract sculptural form.

By the late 1940s McGrath, though performing very creditably in office, had been palpably unlucky in several of the key state projects which might have flexed his architectural muscles. One of his assistants in the late 1940s commented on his uncommon shyness, even as chief architect. Among the keys to his personality were emotional vulnerability and lack of aggressive drive, concealed somewhat in this case by a searching intelligence and by calmness of demeanour. His creative self-belief needed the encouragement of others and the validation of his own success.

Formation of State identity

These were by no means the last of the setbacks McGrath endured. The embassy projects of the 1950s were more consistently successful but do not appear to have risen to the aesthetic levels that were within his capacity. In the early years of the Irish Republic (declared in 1949), it is hard to know whether anyone could have carried off such commissions with the highest and most exacting sense of radical aesthetics. The formation of state identity was always conservative, and the problem of representation was perhaps impossible fully to overcome. Since the 1830s there have been attempts (more or less crude) to establish a valid iconography of 'Irishness' and, for all its artistic successes, even the Gaelic Revival (1890-1910) failed in this regard. In fact it is doubtful if any 20th century artist in any medium has solved the essential problem (in Ireland or elsewhere).

Distinguished diplomatic interiors

Where McGrath had thrived on the serendipitous use of exotic materials during the 1930s, he was now confined to period-décor and a narrow range of native products (sound as they usually were). Within these constraints he did well and the interior designs in London, Paris, Rome and later in Washington, served their purposes excellently. McGrath selected and purchased the London embassy in 1952. The purchase-price of the Paris embassy (the Hotel de Breteuil, on Avenue Foch), alarmed the Dail in 1954 but the building has more than proved its worth. The house was furnished in French period style flavoured by the use of Irish linen, upholstery, carpets, cutlery and glassware.

Villa Spada, Rome

Throughout the 1950s McGrath was occupied with the sensitive refurbishment of the Villa Spada in Rome, which housed the Irish representation to the Vatican. This palazzo was a particular favourite among his charges: a languid unpublished article recounts the pleasures of getting the colouring right on the stuccoed outside walls: the painter was saddened one afternoon by the realisation that 'he can never hope to make the villa more beautiful than it is now'.

Designs State carpets

The most distinctive feature in each of these works of interior design was the set of customised state carpets, which McGrath began to work on from the late 1940s. The first of the hand-knotted Donegal carpets designed by McGrath, adopting Celtic interlocking knotwork as its principal motif, was undertaken for the London embassy in 1952. Others incorporated images of the heads of the river deities (by Edward Smyth) from the Custom House. Several, including those in the Paris embassy, drew inspiration from the classic work of the Savonnerie factory of the late 18th century. These were gorgeous works deeply appropriate to the needs of the contemporary state but McGrath accepted that designs in more modern style may have worked in other contexts.

Awarded RIAI medal

In 1961, having revised Glass in Architecture, he was elected fellow of the Society of Industrial Artists. McGrath, Oscar Richardson and J.B. Maguire collaborated between 1961 and 1968 on the refurbishment of the State Apartments in Dublin Castle: this eventually led to the award of a silver medal for architectural merit from the Royal Institute of the Architects of Ireland.

The Kennedy Hall

For most of the second half of the 1960s McGrath's energies were diverted into a forlorn attempt to bring into being his designs for the ill-fated Kennedy Memorial Hall (the old project of the National Concert Hall revived in new guise in 1964). This project went through many painful twists and turns during the late 1960s and early 1970s before petering out in early 1973. Though it is difficult to pass judgement on something for which he had so much enthusiasm but that did not actually go beyond the design stage (in which it took different shapes) the architectural and popular consensus has not been kind towards his ideas.

Continues to paint and draw

Though he painted a great deal in the 1920s and 1930s (some 138 drawings, engravings and paintings) he showed little publicly. Between 1940 and 1976 he produced about 240 paintings (mostly in watercolour) and pen-and-ink sketches. During the 1940s and 1950s the subjects were mainly Irish in theme. Most of those done in the 1960s and 1970s described continental landscape or architecture. All of this work was figurative. Some 83 of these paintings were exhibited in Dublin in his lifetime (thirty or forty more were shown posthumously in Dublin and in Australia).

Distinction in retirement

McGrath retired from the OPW in May 1968. In the next few years he designed the first scheme for the RHA Gallagher Gallery on Ely Place and built 'Southwood', his first domestic dwelling in Ireland. In 1973 it was largely the benevolence of his personality that assisted in the successful establishment of the Society of Designers of Ireland (he acted as the first President). Having been made associate member of the Royal Hibernian Academy in 1949, he had been elected full Member in 1967 and served as President for the last two months of his life in late 1977. In January 1975, while suffering from the liver cancer which killed him, he noted in a journal that there was 'a rim of warm light on Killiney Hill, the promise of sunshine and a continuation of this premature spring... cold brought tears to the eyes but it was a day one wanted to enjoy'. He died at home in his sleep on 2nd December 1977.

Raymond McGrath, *Twentieth Century Houses* (London, 1934); Raymond McGrath and A.C. Frost, *Glass in Architecture and Design* (London, 1937 and 1961); Alan Powers, 'Simple Intime – the work of Raymond McGrath', *Thirties Society Journal*, no.3 (1982); Nicholas Sheaff, 'The harp re-strung', *Irish Arts Review*, Autumn 1984, pp.37-42; Angela Rolfe, *'Raymond McGrath' Parts 1 and 2 Corridor supplements,* December 1984 and February 1985; Donal O'Donovan, *God's architect: a life of Raymond McGrath* (Dublin, 1995); Raymond McGrath papers, Irish Architectural Archive.

McGrath's pen and ink sketches such as this of Venice, often embellished his personal greetings cards (Courtesy Irish Architectural Archive)